ARMY BOYS IN THE FRENCH TRENCHES

OR, HAND TO HAND FIGHTING WITH THE ENEMY

HOMER RANDALL

Army Boys in the French Trenches

Homer Randall

PO Box 2211
Fairfield, IA 52556
www.1stworldlibrary.com
First Edition

LCCN: 2007934129

Softcover ISBN: 978-1-4218-9650-2
Hardcover ISBN: 978-1-4218-9750-9
eBook ISBN: 978-1-4218-9550-5

1st World Library Literary Society

Giving Back to the World

"If you want to work on the core problem, it's early school literacy."

- James Barksdale, former CEO of Netscape

"No skill is more crucial to the future of a child, or to a democratic and prosperous society, than literacy."

- Los Angeles Times

"Literacy... means far more than learning how to read and write... The aim is to transmit... knowledge and promote social participation."

- UNESCO

"Literacy is not a luxury, it is a right and a responsibility. If our world is to meet the challenges of the twenty-first century we must harness the energy and creativity of all our citizens."

- President Bill Clinton

"Parents should be encouraged to read to their children, and teachers should be equipped with all available techniques for teaching literacy, so the varying needs and capacities of individual kids can be taken into account."

- Hugh Mackay

CONTENTS

CHAPTER I

A SLASHING ATTACK

"Stand ready, boys. We attack at dawn!"

The word passed in a whisper down the long line of the trench, where the American army boys crouched like so many khaki-clad ghosts, awaiting the command to go "over the top."

"That will be in about fifteen minutes from now, I figure," murmured Frank Sheldon to his friend and comrade, Bart Raymond, as he glanced at the hands of his radio watch and then put it up to his ear to make sure that it had not stopped.

"It'll seem more like fifteen hours," muttered Tom Bradford, who was on the other side of Sheldon.

"Tom's in a hurry to get at the Huns," chuckled Billy Waldon. "He wants to show them where they get off."

"I saw him putting a razor edge on his bayonet last night," added Bart. "Now he's anxious to see how it works."

"He'll have plenty of chances to find out," said Frank. "This is going to be a hot scrap, or I miss my guess. I heard the captain tell the lieutenant that the Germans had their heaviest force right in front of our part of the line."

"So much the better," asserted Billy stoutly. "They can't come too thick or too fast. They've been sneering at what the Yankees were going to do in this war, and it's about time they got punctures in their tires."

At this moment the mess helpers passed along the line with buckets of steaming hot coffee, and the men welcomed it eagerly, for it was late in the autumn and the night air was chill and penetrating. "Come, little cup, to one who loves thee well," murmured Tom, as he swallowed his portion in one gulp.

The others were not slow in following his example, and the buckets were emptied in a twinkling.

Then the stern vigil was renewed.

From the opposing lines a star shell rose and exploded, casting a greenish radiance over the barren stretch of No Man's Land that separated the hostile forces.

"Fritz isn't asleep," muttered Frank.

"He's right on the job with his fireworks," agreed Bart.

"Maybe he has his suspicions that we're going to give him a little surprise party," remarked Billy, "and that's his way of telling us that he's ready to welcome us with open arms."

"Fix bayonets!" came the command from the officer in charge, and there was a faint clink as the order was obeyed.

"It won't be long now," murmured Tom. "But why don't the

guns open up?"

"They always do before it's time to charge," commented Billy, as he shifted his position a little. "I suppose they will now almost any minute."

"I don't think there'll be any gun fire this time before we go over the top," ventured Frank.

"What do you mean?" asked Bart in surprise, as he turned his head toward his chum.

"Do you know anything?" queried Tom.

"Not exactly know, but I've heard enough to make a guess," replied Frank. "I think we're going to play the game a little differently this time. Unless I'm mistaken, the Huns are going to get the surprise of their lives."

"Put on gas masks!" came another order, and in the six seconds allowed for this operation the masks were donned, making the men in the long line look like so many goblins.

It was light enough for them to see each other now, for the gray fingers of the dawn were already drawing the curtain of darkness aside from the eastern sky.

One minute more passed—a minute of tense, fierce expectation, while the boys gripped their rifles until it seemed that their fingers would bury themselves in the stocks.

Crash!

With a roar louder than a thousand guns the earth under the German first-line trenches split asunder, and tons of rock and mud and guns and men were hurled toward the sky.

The din was terrific, the sight appalling, and the shock for an instant was almost as great to the Americans as to their opponents, though far less tragic.

"Now, men," shouted their lieutenant, "over with you!" and with a wild yell of exultation the boys clambered over the edge of the trench and started toward the German lines.

"We're off!" panted Frank, as, with eyes blazing and bayonet ready for instant use, he rushed forward in the front rank.

"To a flying start!" gasped Bart, and then because breath was precious they said no more, but raced on like greyhounds freed from the leash.

On, on they went, with the wind whipping their faces! On, still on, to the red ruin wrought by the explosion of the mine.

For the first fifty yards the going was easy except for the craters and shell holes into which some of the boys slid and tumbled. The enemy had been so numbed and paralyzed by the overwhelming explosion that they seemed to be unable to make any resistance.

But the officers knew, and the men as well, that this was only the lull before the storm. Their enemy was desperate and resourceful, and though the cleverness of the American engineers had carried through the mine operation without detection, it was certain that the foe would rally.

Fifty yards from the first-line trench—forty—thirty—and then the German guns spoke.

A long line of flame flared up crimson in the pallid dawn.

"Down, men, down!" shouted their officers, and the Yankee

lads threw themselves flat on the ground while a leaden hail swept furiously over them.

"Are you hurt, Bart?" cried Frank anxiously, as he heard a sharp exclamation from his comrade.

"Not by a bullet," growled Bart. "Took some of the skin off my knee though when I went down."

A second time the murderous fire came hurtling over them, but the officers noted with satisfaction that the enemy were shooting high.

"They haven't got the range yet," observed Billy.

"Up!" came the word of command, and again the men were on their feet and racing like mad toward the trench.

They came at last to where it had been. For it was no longer a trench!

Gone was the zigzag line that the boys knew by heart from having faced and fought against it for weeks. The mine had done its work thoroughly.

Everywhere was a welter of hideous confusion. Barbed wire entanglements with their supporting posts had been rooted from the ground. Guns had been torn from their carriages. "Pill boxes" had been smashed to bits. Horses and men and wagons and camp kitchens were mingled together in wildest chaos.

Parts of the trench had been filled to the surface with earth, while huge boulders blocked the entrance to some of the communicating passages.

There were a few sharp fights with scattered units of the enemy that had retained their senses and were trying to get their machine guns into action. But these detachments were soon cut down or captured. The great majority of the survivors were so dazed that they surrendered with scarcely a show of resistance and were rounded up in squads to be sent to the rear.

The first trench had been won, and it was almost a bloodless victory, only a few of the American troops having fallen in the sudden rush.

But sterner work lay ahead, for the second and third German lines were still intact, bristling with men and supported heavily by their guns.

"This was easy," grinned Billy.

"Like taking a dead mouse from a blind kitten," chuckled Tom, as he wiped the grime and perspiration from his face.

"Don't fool yourselves," warned Frank, as a shell came whining over their heads. "This was only a skirmish. The real fight is coming, and coming mighty quick!"

CHAPTER II

THE UPLIFTED KNIFE

Even while Frank Sheldon spoke, the artillery of the enemy took on a deeper note until it reached the intensity of drumfire.

But now the American gunners took a hand, and the shells came pouring over the heads of the boys, searching out the line of the second enemy trench and preparing the way for the advance.

In obedience to commands, the American soldiers had sought shelter wherever they could find it, while they were recovering their wind.

Only a moment could be granted for this, however, for time was everything just now. They had caught the enemy off his guard and must take advantage of the opportunity.

"Line up, men!" cried the leader of Frank's detachment, and the high state of discipline that the American forces had reached was shown by the promptness with which the order was obeyed.

A signal was sent back to the supporting guns, and they

opened up a deadly barrage fire over the heads of Frank and his comrades, clearing the ground before them of everything that dared to show itself in the open.

Behind this curtain of fire, the boys advanced, slowly at first, but gathering speed at every stride, until they were running at the double quick.

Bullets rained about them from the machine guns of the enemy and great shells tore gaps in the ranks. At Frank's left, a soldier suddenly wavered and then pitched headlong into a shell hole and lay still. Another toppled over with a bullet in his shoulder. But the lanes that were made closed almost instantly.

Now they had reached the wire entanglements that had been battered by the artillery until they hung in festoons around their posts, leaving paths through which the American lads poured.

Then like a great tidal wave they struck the trench!

The Germans had clambered out to meet them, and when the two forces met the shock was terrific. Back and forth the battle surged and swayed, each side fighting with the fury of desperation. The cannon had ceased now, for in that locked mass the shells were as likely to kill friends as foes. It was man against man, bayonet against bayonet, each combatant obeying the primitive law of "kill or be killed."

The opposing forces at this part of the line were nearly equal, with the Germans having a slight advantage in numbers. But to make up for this, the Americans had the advantage of the attack and the tremendous momentum with which they had struck the enemy's line.

For a time victory hung in the balance, but then Yankee determination and superior skill in bayonet work began to tell. The Americans would not be denied. The German line was pierced, and the forces broke up into a number of battling groups.

Frank and Bart, Billy and Tom, who all through the fight had managed to keep together, found themselves engaged with a squad of Germans double their number, two of whom were frantically trying to bring a machine gun to bear upon them.

With a bound Frank was upon them. He toppled one over with his bayonet, but while he was doing this the other fired at him point-blank with a revolver. At such a close range he could not have missed, had not Bart, quick as a flash, clubbed him over the arm with his rifle, making the bullet go wild.

"Quick, Bart!" panted Frank, as with his comrade's help he slued the machine gun around, gripped the trigger, and sent a stream of bullets into a group of the enemy charging down upon him.

Before that withering fire they dissolved like mist, and a circle was cleared as though by magic.

What Germans were left in that immediate vicinity leaped back into the trench on the edge of which they had been fighting.

"Now we've got them!" cried Frank, as with his friends' assistance he quickly wheeled the gun to the brink of the trench and depressed the muzzle so that it commanded the huddled bunch below. "Come out of that, you fellows. Hands up, quick!"

They may not have understood his words, but there was no misunderstanding the meaning of that black sinister muzzle of the machine gun with a hundred deaths behind it. They were trapped, and their hands went up with cries of "*Kamerad!*" in token of surrender.

On that part of the line the battle was over, for the plan did not contemplate going beyond the second trench at that time. The American boys had won and won gloriously. From all parts of the trench, on a two-mile front, groups of captives were coming sullenly out with uplifted hands, to be herded into groups by their captors and sent to the rear.

"Glory hallelujah!" cried Bart, as he removed his mask and wiped his streaming face. "And no gas, either."

"Some scrap!" gasped Billy, as he sank exhausted to the ground.

"Did them up to the Queen's taste," chuckled Tom.

"We certainly put one over on the Huns that time," grinned Frank happily.

And while they stand there, breathless and exulting, it may be well for the benefit of those who have not previously made the acquaintance of the American Army Boys to sketch briefly their adventures up to the time this story opens.

Frank Sheldon, Bart Raymond, Tom Bradford and Billy Waldon had all been born and brought up in Camport, a thriving American city of about twenty-five thousand people. They had known each other from boyhood, attended the same school, played on the same baseball nine and were warm friends.

Frank was the natural leader of the group. He was a tall, muscular young fellow, quick to think and quick to act, always at the front in sports as well as in the more serious events of life.

His father had died some years before, leaving only a modest home as a legacy, and Frank was the sole support of his mother. The latter had been born in France, where Mr. Sheldon had married her and brought her to America.

Later, Mrs. Sheldon's father had died, leaving her a considerable property in Auvergne, her native province. This estate, however, had been tied up in a lawsuit, and she had not come into possession of it. She had been planning to go to France to look after her interests, but her husband's death and, later on, the breaking out of the European war, had made this impossible.

She was a charming woman, with all the French sparkle and vivacity, and she and her son were bound together in ties of the strongest affection. Naturally her ardent sympathy had been with France in the great war raging in Europe. But when it became evident that America soon would take part, although she welcomed the aid this would bring to her native country, her mother heart was torn with anguish at the thought that her only son would probably join in the fighting across the sea.

But Frank, though he dreaded the separation, felt that he must join the Camport regiment that was getting ready to fight the Huns. The deciding moment came when a German tore down the American flag from a neighbor's porch. Frank knocked the fellow down and in the presence of an excited throng made him kiss the flag that he had insulted. From that moment his resolution was taken, and his mother, who had witnessed the scene, gave her consent to his joining the old

Thirty-seventh regiment, made up chiefly of Camport boys, including Billy Waldon, who had seen service on the Mexican border.

Bart Raymond, Frank's special chum, a sturdy, vigorous young fellow, was equally patriotic, and joined the regiment with Frank as soon as war was declared. Tom Bradford, a fellow employee in the firm of Moore & Thomas, a thriving hardware house, wanted to enlist, but was rejected on account of his teeth, although he wrathfully declared that "he wanted to shoot the Germans, not to bite them." In fact, almost all the young fellows employed by the firm, except "Reddy," the office boy, who wanted to go badly enough, but who was too young, tried to get into some branch of the army or navy.

A marked exception was Nick Rabig, the foreman of the shipping department, who, although born in the United States, came of German parents and lost no opportunity of "boosting" Germany and "knocking" America. He was the bully of the place and universally disliked. He hated Frank, especially after the flag incident, and only the thought of his mother had prevented Frank more than once from giving Rabig the thrashing he deserved.

Frank's regiment was sent to Camp Boone for their preliminary training, and here the young recruits were put through their paces in rifle shooting, grenade throwing, bayonet practice and all the other exercises by which Uncle Sam turns his boys into soldiers. There was plenty of fun mixed in with the hard work, and they had many stirring experiences. A pleasant feature was the coming of Tom, who although rejected when he tried to enlist had been accepted in the draft. Not so pleasant, though somewhat amusing, was the fact that Nick Rabig also had been drafted and had to go to Camp Boone, though most unwillingly.

How the regiment sailed to France for intensive training behind the firing lines; how their transport narrowly escaped being sunk by a submarine and how the tables were turned; the singular chance by which Frank met a French colonel and heard encouraging news about his mother's property; how he thoroughly "trimmed" Rabig in a boxing bout; how the Camport boys took part in the capture of a Zeppelin; how the old Thirty-seventh finally reached the trenches; Frank's daring exploit when caught in the swirl of a German charge; these and other exciting adventures are told in the first book of this Series, entitled: "Army Boys in France; Or, From Training Camp to the Trenches."

"Do you remember what that airship captain said the day we bagged him?" chuckled Billy.

"About it being impossible for Americans to get to France?" asked Bart. "You bet I do. I'll never forget that boob. I wonder if he still believes it."

"He'd sing a different tune if he were here to-day," observed Tom.

"I don't know," laughed Frank. "The German skull is pretty thick. Still you can get something through it once in a while if you keep on hammering."

"I guess these fellows haven't any doubts about our being here," observed Billy.

"They've had pretty good evidence of it," confirmed Tom, as he watched the enemy captives standing about in dejected groups, waiting to be sent to the rear.

One thing that struck the boys forcibly was the disparity of age between the prisoners. There was an unusual proportion of men beyond middle life and of youngsters still in their teens.

"Grandpas and kids," blurted out Tom.

"The Kaiser's robbing the cradle and the grave," commented Billy. "Germany's getting pretty near to the limit of her man power, I guess."

"That's true of France and England, too," observed Frank thoughtfully. "They lost the flower of their troops in the early fighting and they all have to do a great deal of combing to keep their ranks full."

"And that's where America has the Indian sign on the Huns," jubilated Bart "We'll have our best against her second best."

"We'll trim her good and proper," predicted Frank. "Even at her best, we'd down her in the end. But don't let's kid ourselves. She's full of fight yet, and will take a lot of beating. And there are plenty of huskies in her ranks yet. Look at that big brute over there. He looks as though he could lift an ox."

He pointed to a massively built German corporal, who was evidently mad with rage at his capture. He was gesticulating wildly to his fellow prisoners and fairly sputtering in the attempt to relieve his feelings.

"Seems to be rather peeved," grinned Tom.

"I can't catch on to what he's saying," laughed Bart. "But I'll bet he could give points to a New York truckman or the mate of a Mississippi steamboat. They'd turn green with envy if they could understand him."

"He's frothing at the mouth," chuckled Billy. "I'd hate to

have him bite me just now. I'd get hydrophobia sure."

There was no time for further comment. The officers had had to give the men a short breathing spell, for all were spent with their tremendous exertions. But now after the brief rest, all was bustle and hurry.

"The Huns will be back for more," predicted Frank, as he and his friends were set to work changing the sandbags from the side of the trench that had faced the Americans to the other side that looked toward the German third line.

"They must be hard to please if they haven't had enough for one morning," growled Tom.

"They're gluttons for punishment," remarked Bart. "The first-line trench is junk from the mine explosion, but they won't give this second one up without making one mighty effort to get it back."

The young soldiers were working feverishly to organize the captured position, when their corporal, Wilson, summoned them out and they scrambled forth promptly and stood at attention.

"Fall in to take back the prisoners," he ordered.

A look of disappointment came over their faces and Wilson's eyes twinkled when he saw it.

"Haven't you had enough fighting yet?" he demanded. "Well, I feel that way myself, but orders are orders. Come along."

"Hard luck," muttered Frank in a low tone to Bart, as they obeyed the command.

"We'll miss some lovely fighting," agreed Bart.

"I was just getting warmed up," mourned Billy.

"Don't worry," advised Tom. "We'll be sent back after we get these fellows to headquarters, and we'll have a chance to get another crack at them."

The prisoners, having been searched, were placed in double file between the members of the guarding squad, who walked at a few paces interval on either side of them.

"Fall in!" came the corporal's order. "Shoulder arms. March!"

They started out briskly.

Frank and Bart happened to be close beside the big German corporal whom they had before observed. His wrath was not yet abated, and he kept up a volley of epithets as he sullenly marched along.

"He's making as much fuss as though he were the Kaiser," chuckled Tom, who was vastly amused at the prisoner's antics.

"Slap him on the wrist and tell him to be nice," counseled Billy with a grin.

The captive glared at them with insane rage in his eyes.

"I think he's going nutty," remarked Bart. "It's lucky for him there aren't any squirrels around."

"You want to keep your eye peeled for him," warned Frank. "He's bad medicine."

"He's safe enough," replied Bart, carelessly. "He hasn't any weapon, and if he started to run he wouldn't get far. He isn't cut out for a sprinter."

"Even if he were, a bullet would catch him," chimed in Billy. "He'd make a big target and it would be a pretty bad shot that would miss him."

When they reached the blown-up first trench they found it difficult to keep in line, and had to pick their way over the heaped-up ruin that had been made by the mine explosion.

Bart tripped over a strand of broken wire, and in trying to save himself from falling, his rifle slipped from his hand.

The German corporal was within a foot of him and saw his opportunity.

Quick as a flash he drew from his clothing a trench knife that the searchers had overlooked. The murderous blade gleamed in the air as the corporal brought it down toward the neck of Bart, who had stooped to pick up his rifle.

CHAPTER III

TAKING CHANCES

"Look out, Bart!" yelled Billy, while Tom made a desperate leap to his comrade's rescue.

But Frank was quicker than either.

Like lightning he lunged with his bayonet and caught the German in the wrist, just as the knife was about to bury itself in Bart's neck.

With a howl of rage and pain, as his arm was forced upward, the prisoner's hand lost its grip on the weapon and it clattered harmlessly to the ground.

In an instant the German was overpowered and his arms tied behind him with his own belt. Then his wounded wrist was bound up with a surgical dressing, and under a special guard he was urged forward in no gentle manner, for all were at a white heat at his treacherous attempt.

By the laws of war his life was forfeited, and he seemed to realize this, for all his bravado vanished and from time to time he looked fearfully at his captors. He saw little there to encourage him, for Bart was a great favorite with his company and the attack had stirred them to the depths.

"A close call, old man." said Frank, affectionately tapping his friend on the shoulder. "It would have been taps for me, all right, if you hadn't acted as quickly as you did," responded Bart gratefully.

"Frank was Johnny-on-the-spot," said Billy admiringly. "My heart was in my mouth when I saw that knife coming down."

"It was a waste of time to tie up that fellow's arm," remarked Tom, as he glowered at the miscreant. "He'll soon be where he won't need any bandages."

"I guess it's a case for a firing squad," judged Billy. "But it serves him right, for it was up to him to play the game."

Before long they reached headquarters and delivered up their prisoners. If they had expected to be sent back immediately to the firing line, they were disappointed, for the examination of the prisoners began at once, without the squad receiving notice of dismissal.

This had its compensations, however, for although they had captured prisoners before, they had never been present at their examination, and they were curious to see the turn the questioning would take.

Captain Baker, of the old Thirty-seventh, was detailed to do the examining, and because time was precious and it was most important to learn just what enemy units were opposed to the American forces, he got to work at once, an interpreter standing at his side while a stenographer made note of the replies.

The captain signaled to one of the most intelligent looking of the prisoners, and the latter stepped out, clicked his heels together smartly and saluted.

"What is your name?" asked the captain.

"Rudolph Schmidt."

"Your regiment?"

"The Seventy-ninth Bavarian."

"Who is your colonel?"

"Von Armin."

"Who commands your division?"

"General Hofer."

"Who is your corps commander?"

"Prince Lichtenstein."

"How many men have you lost in the last few days' fighting?"

Obstinate silence.

The captain repeated the question.

"I do not know," the prisoner answered evasively.

"Well, were your losses heavy or light?" pursued the captain patiently.

"I cannot tell."

The captain switched to another line.

"Do you know who have captured you?" he asked.

"The English," was the prompt answer.

"No," replied the captain. "We are Americans."

The prisoner permitted himself an incredulous smile.

"Can't you see these are American uniforms?" asked the captain, with a sweep of his arm.

"Yes," was the reply. "But our captain tells us that the English wear that uniform to make us think that the Americans have arrived in France."

A grin went around the circle of listeners.

"You blawsted, bloody Britisher," chuckled Bart, giving Frank a poke in the ribs.

"Where's my bally monocle, old top?" whispered Frank, while Billy and Tom grew red in the face from trying to control their merriment.

The captain himself had all he could do to maintain his gravity.

"Do you believe your captain when he tells you that?" he inquired.

"I must believe him," answered the prisoner simply.

"There's discipline for you," muttered Billy.

"Such childlike faith," murmured Tom.

"But even if the Americans are not already here," persisted the captain, "don't you believe they are coming?"

"They may try to come," answered the captive doubtfully; "but if they do, they will never get here."

"Why not."

"Our U-boats will stop them."

"That settles it," whispered Bart. "We think we're here, but we're only kidding ourselves. We *can't* be here. Heinie says so and, of course, he knows."

"What a come-on he'd be for the confidence men," gurgled Billy. "They'd sell him the Brooklyn Bridge before he'd been on shore for an hour."

Questioned as to food supplies, the German admitted that their rations, although fairly good, were not so abundant as at the beginning of the war. Then with characteristic arrogance he added:

"But we will have plenty to eat and drink too when we get to Paris."

"I suppose your captain tells you that too," remarked the inquisitor.

"Yes," was the reply.

"That eternal captain again," murmured Bart.

"He must be a wonder," chuckled Tom.

"You've been rather a long time on the road to Paris, haven't you?" asked the captain, with a tinge of sarcasm. "Seems to me I've heard something about a banquet that was to celebrate the Crown Prince's entry into Paris a month after the war was started."

A discomfited look stole over the prisoner's face.

"That was Von Kluck's fault," he said sullenly.

"Seems to me the French army had something to do with it too," whispered Frank to Bart. "What does your captain tell you your armies are fighting for?" continued the questioner.

"To give Germany her place in the sun," answered the prisoner without hesitation.

"That seems to be a stock phrase of the Huns," whispered Billy. "I'll bet it's part of the lesson taught in every German school."

A few more questions followed, but failed to elicit any information of special importance, and the prisoner was dismissed, to have his place taken by some of his comrades.

But what they told the boys never knew, for just then Corporal Wilson, who had been in close conference with his lieutenant, beckoned to them and they filed silently out of the quarters.

"Back to the firing line for us," remarked Frank.

"About time too," replied Bart, as he shouldered his rifle. "We've been missing all the fun."

But the first words of the corporal showed them that they

were mistaken.

"You lads are out of it for the rest of the day," he remarked. "Go back to your old trench now, get some grub and tumble into your bunks."

They looked at each other in surprise, for the sun had not much more than risen.

"You heard what I said," reiterated the corporal. "Get all the sleep you can to-day, for you won't do any sleeping to-night!"

CHAPTER IV

BETWEEN THE LINES

The Army boys looked at each other in blank inquiry, but the corporal did not offer to enlighten them, and they were too good soldiers to ask questions when orders were given.

"What do you suppose is in the wind now?" asked Bart, as they made their way to their sleeping quarters.

"Search me," replied Frank.

"Aeroplanes," chirped Billy.

Bart made a thrust at him which Billy dodged.

"I guess we're picked for a scouting party," remarked Tom. "The captain may want to confirm some of the information he's getting from those chaps."

"Information!" snorted Bart. "More likely misinformation. Those fellows struck me as being dandy liars."

"They wouldn't be Huns if they weren't," remarked Billy. "You know Baron Munchausen came from over the Rhine, so they come rightly by their talent in that line. But what's the matter with Tony here?" he added, as they passed by one of the field kitchens in a protected nook, where one of the bakers was kneading away desperately at some dough and muttering volubly to himself.

"He seems all riled up about something, for a fact," commented Frank.

"What's the matter, Tony?" inquired Bart of the perspiring baker, an Italian who had spent some years in the United States and who was generally liked by the boys of the old Thirty-seventh because of his customary good nature and his skill in compounding their favorite dishes.

Tony looked up in despair.

"I can't maka de dough," he complained. "I worka more dan hour. It lika de sand. It getta my goat."

The boys laughed at his woe-begone face.

"Put some more water with it," suggested Billy at a venture.

Tony looked at him with such a glare of contempt that the amateur baker wilted.

"I usa de water!" he exclaimed. "Plent water! No maka de stick."

"It looks all right," remarked Frank, as he picked up some of the substance on the kneading board and let it dribble through his fingers, "but as Tony says, it's like so much sand."

"And it tastes queer," said Billy, putting a bit of it on his tongue.

"Looks as though some of the food profiteers were trying to put something over on us," observed Tom.

Just then one of the commissary men came along, evidently looking for something.

"There's a bag of trench foot powder missing," he said. "Have any of you chaps seen anything of it?"

"Not guilty," returned Bart. "Though the way my feet feel it wouldn't do them a bit of harm to have some of that powder on them right now."

A sudden light dawned upon Frank.

"Say, Tony!" he exclaimed, "let's see the bag you got that flour from."

Tony complied and brought forth from one of his receptacles a large paper bag which was two thirds full.

Frank seized it and turned it around to see what was stamped on the other side. Then he almost dropped the bag in a wild fit of hilarity.

"No wonder Tony couldn't make his dough!" he exclaimed, when he could speak. "Some chump in the supply department has handed him out a bag of foot powder when he asked for flour."

He showed the others the marking on the bag, and their merriment equaled his own, while Tony alternately glowered and grinned. He had begun to think that somebody had cast on him the "evil eye," so dreaded by his countrymen, and he was relieved to find that his plight was due to natural causes. Yet the thought of all that wasted effort stirred him to resentment.

"That's one on you, Tony, old boy!" chuckled Billy, with a poke in the ribs.

"It's lucky the dough wouldn't stick," laughed Frank. "There wouldn't have been much nourishment in that kind of bread."

"Dat guy a bonehead," asserted Tony, as he scraped his board with vigor. "A vera beeg bonehead."

The boys assented and passed on laughing.

"And now for grub!" exclaimed Billy. "Oh, boy, maybe it won't taste good!"

"I guess we've earned our breakfast, all right," said Bart.

"I can stand a whole lot of filling up," observed Tom. "Talk about exercise before breakfast to get you an appetite. We've sure had enough of it this morning."

"I never ran so fast in my life," declared Billy. "A Marathon runner would have had nothing on me."

"We must have covered the space between those trenches in about twenty seconds," agreed Bart.

"Well, as long as we weren't running in the wrong direction it was all right," grinned Tom.

"The Boches haven't seen our backs yet, and here's hoping it will be some time before they'll have that treat," said Frank with a laugh.

They ate like famished wolves and then threw themselves on

their bunks to get a long sleep in preparation for the strenuous night that lay before them. And so used had they already become to roaring of cannon and whining of bullets and shrieking of shells, that, although the din was almost incessant all through that day, it bothered them not at all.

It was nearly dusk when the corporal passed along, giving them a shake that roused them from their slumbers and brought them out of their bunks in a hurry.

"Time to get up, boys," said the corporal. "Not that we're going to start out right away. But we've got quite a job before us and I want you to have plenty of time to think over your instructions and have them sink in."

They dressed quickly and after a hearty supper reported to Wilson at their company headquarters.

They found the corporal grave and preoccupied.

"As I suppose you fellows have already guessed," he began, "we're going to-night on a scouting party. We're to find out the condition of the wire in front of that third trench that the Huns still hold, and we want to get more exact information about the location of the enemy's machine guns. Anything else we find out will be welcome, but those are the main things.

"It's going to be pretty risky work," he continued. "Not but what there's always plenty of risk about a job of this kind, but to-night there's more than usual. The fierce fighting to-day has got the enemy all stirred up and he'll be on the alert. Likely enough he'll have scouting parties of his own out, and we may run across them in the dark. Then it will be a question of who is the quicker with knife or bayonet. Now you boys scatter and get your crawling suits and hoods and masks, and we'll be ready for business.

"I can see that there'll be no monotony in our young lives to-night," observed Frank to Bart, as they obeyed instructions.

"Not that you can notice," agreed Bart. "The corp has quite a little program marked out for us."

"So it seems."

"And No Man's Land is going to be a little rougher land to-night than it ever was before," predicted Tom. "That mine explosion hasn't done a thing to it."

"All the better," chimed in Billy. "There'll be better places to hide in when Fritz throws up his star shells. But let's get a hustle on or the corp will be after us."

They got into their "crawling suits," so named because they were used only on scouting duty, when it was necessary to move over the earth on their stomachs or at best on hands and knees. They were a dead black in color, and in addition to the suit itself comprised a black mask and hood. The hood was loose and shapeless, so as to avoid the sharp outline that would have been afforded if it were tight-fitting.

Dressed in this fashion and lying prone and motionless on the ground whenever a star shell threw its greenish radiance over the field, the scouts were reasonably safe from detection and sniping. They would seem, if seen at all, to be just so many more objects added to the hundreds that littered up the ground between the two armies.

Since they had been in France, the boys had had special training in scouting duty, and the one thing that had been drilled into them perhaps more than anything else was the necessity for "playing dead," as Tom expressed it. One of their exercises compelled them to lie on the ground absolutely motionless for an hour. Not even a muscle could twitch without bringing a reprimand from their keen-eyed instructor. Another part of the drill made them take half an hour merely to rise to their feet from a prostrate position, each move in the process being marked by the utmost caution. It was hard drill, but necessary, and in time the boys had gained a control over their muscles that would have done credit to an Apache Indian.

In a few minutes they were fully arrayed in their crawling suits and reported to Corporal Wilson. He looked them over carefully and noted with satisfaction that nothing that was essential to the success of their night foray was lacking.

"With a fair share of luck we'll bring home the bacon," he remarked, as he led the way from the trench.

At the start there was no special caution necessary, as would have been the case the day before. For the two trenches in front of them that had been occupied by the enemy were now in the possession of the United States troops.

All that day, since the mine explosion had given the signal for attack and storm, the Germans who had been driven from their first two lines of trenches had made desperate efforts to get them back. There had been fierce counter attacks, many times repeated, but through them all the Americans had stood like a rock and thrown the enemy back without yielding a foot of the conquered ground.

At nightfall the enemy had ceased his infantry attacks, although the big guns on both sides, like angry mastiffs, kept growling at each other.

"It's been a great day for our fellows," exulted Frank, as they picked their way through the welter of debris that bore testimony to the violence of the fighting.

"It sure has," agreed Bart.

"We've got there with both feet," remarked Tom.

"And in both trenches," chimed in Billy.

"Yes," said Frank. "I'm glad we didn't stop at the first one. The mine caught the Boches napping there and stood them on their heads. But in the second it was an out and out stand up fight, man to man, and we licked them."

"And licked them good," asserted Billy. "I guess they won't do any more sneering at the Yankees after this day's work."

They passed the place where Bart had so nearly met his death through the treacherous attack of his captive.

"Here's where you nearly went West," remarked Tom.

"Don't talk of it," objected Bart with a grimace. "It makes the chills creep over me to think of it. I could stand being knifed in a square fight, but I'd hate to get it the way that fellow meant that I should."

"One of the Frenchmen was telling me of something like that that happened at Verdun," said Frank. 'Two Frenchmen were carrying a wounded German officer on a stretcher to the hospital. The officer got out his revolver and shot the first stretcher bearer dead."

"That's gratitude for you," remarked Bart. "Something like another German in a hospital, who pretended he wanted to shake hands with the Red Cross nurse who was tending him, and then with a sudden snap broke her wrist."

"You hear it said sometimes," said Billy, "that 'the only good Indian is a dead Indian.' That's always sounded a little tough on poor Lo. But if the Huns keep on the way they are going, it won't be long before all the world will be saying that the only good German is a dead one."

"I'm beginning to say it already," replied Tom.

They passed stretcher bearers carrying away the wounded, and burial parties engaged in a business still more sad. There was plenty for them to do, for death and wounds had come to many that day, which had been the most strenuous for the United States troops since they had come to the fighting line.

That many of their regiment had fallen and still more been wounded the boys knew well, although the full toll of their losses would not be known until the next day. But the enemy had lost still more, and a large number of prisoners were in American hands. They had taken two trenches on a wide front, and that night American boys were eating their suppers in the dugouts where Germans had breakfasted in the morning. It had been a dashing attack with a successful result, and Uncle Sam had reason to be proud of his nephews.

"One more step on the road to the Rhine," exulted Frank, voicing the thought that stirred them all.

"Right you are," replied Bart "It's a long, long road, but we'll get there."

"Do you remember what old Peterson said just before we left for France?" queried Tom. "'The United States has put her hand to the plow and she won't turn back.'"

"Good old Peterson!" remarked Billy. "He was a dandy scrapper himself in the old days when he wore the blue. I'll bet he's rooting for us every day."

"Sure he is," agreed Frank. "Everybody in the old firm is."

"Reddy's rooting the hardest of them all," laughed Bart, referring to the red-headed office boy. "Do you remember how excited the little rascal got when the old Thirty-seventh went past? He almost tumbled out of the window. And how he cheered!"

"He's got the right stuff in him," said Tom. "Do you know, I shouldn't be a bit surprised to see that kid turn up here some time."

"You're dreaming," replied Bart.

"You wait and see," prophesied Tom. "When any one wants a thing hard enough he usually gets it. He'll ship as cabin boy or something of the kind and some day, when we're least expecting it, Reddy will pop up here. Watch my hunch."

"How scared the Huns would be if they knew that Reddy was coming to clean them up," mocked Tom.

"He might account for some of them at that," remarked Billy. "A bullet from Reddy's gun would go as fast and hit as hard as any other. You know what David did to Goliath."

By this time they had passed the second captured trench and were facing the enemy's trench about three hundred yards away. Their talk ceased or died down to whispers.

Before them stretched the desolate waste of No Man's Land, pitted with shell holes, blasted and seared by the pitiless storm of fire that had swept it all that day.

Once it had been fertile and beautiful. Now it was withered and hideous. It was a grim commentary on the war that had been as ruthless toward nature as it had been toward man.

"Now, boys," said the corporal in a low voice, "you know what we've got to do. Keep together as much as you can and —Drop!"

The last command came out like a shot, and was caused by a star shell that rose from the opposing trench and burst in a flood of greenish light.

Had they been standing, it would have revealed them clearly, but at their leader's word they had dropped instantly to the ground, where they lay motionless until the light died away.

Then they rose and like so many shadows moved cautiously forward, with a motion more like drifting than walking, their ears alert, their eyes strained, their hearts beating fast with excitement.

CHAPTER V

THE BARBAROUS HUNS

The night was as black as pitch, which, while an advantage in one way, was a disadvantage in another. For though it lessened their chance of detection, it also made it more difficult to get the lay of the land and keep their sense of direction.

But here again their training came into play, for they had been specially drilled to be blindfolded and remain in that condition for hours at a time. In that way they had developed their sense of feeling just as a blind man does and had acquired an almost uncanny ability to avoid obstacles and steer a course without the aid of their eyes.

"Gee!" whispered Bart to Frank, as the two comrades moved along side by side, "I never saw a night so dark."

"Yes," replied his comrade, "it's as black as velvet. You could almost cut it with a knife."

"Lucky if that's the only cutting we'll have to do before the night is over," murmured Tom.

Soon they reached a little patch of woodland that stood

almost halfway between the lines. Only a few gaunt trees had been left standing, mere skeletons of what they had been, every branch and twig swept away by shells and bullets and even the bark stripped off, leaving the trunks in ghastly nakedness.

But they still afforded shelter from bursting shrapnel or a sniper's bullet, and the boys stood behind them for a few moments while they listened intently for any sound that might betray the presence of an enemy patrol, prowling about on an errand similar to their own.

But nothing suspicious developed, and, reassured, they again, at a signal from their leader, moved forward. But new they were no longer on their feet. They were too close to the German line for that.

Down on hands and knees they wormed their way along inch by inch, reaching out their hand cautiously for each fresh grip on the uneven ground. Sometimes their hands encountered emptiness and they were warned that they were on the edge of a shell hole. At other times they drew back in instinctive repulsion, as they felt the rigid outlines of a dead body. But whatever detours they had to make, they managed by touch or whisper to keep together, and although their progress was slow it was still progress, and they knew that they were steadily nearing the German lines.

Suddenly Frank's extended hand came in contact with a sharp object that he recognized on the instant. It was the barb on a broken strand of wire.

They had reached the entanglement protecting a segment of the German trench.

Frank had been a trifle in advance of his comrades, and he

softly signaled his discovery to the others. In an instant they had stiffened out and lay as rigid as statues.

For five minutes not one of them stirred, while they listened for the tread of the sentry who might be stationed behind the wires.

Some distance off they could hear the sound of voices in guttural tones, the occasional click of a bayonet as it was slipped into place, the low rumble of what might have been field pieces being moved into position.

Now too their eyes came into play, for ahead of them the darkness was threaded with a faint ray of light that rose above the trench, and while it did little more than make darkness visible, it was still sufficient to form a background against which they could have detected the figure of a sentinel.

But they drew no false assurance from that fact, for the enemy's patrol might be lying on the ground, as silent as themselves and as watchful, ready to fire in the direction of the slightest sound.

It was a nerve-trying situation, but life or death might depend on their self-control, and they stood the test successfully, although poor Tom had an almost irrepressible desire to sneeze, in conquering which he almost broke a blood vessel.

Convinced at last that it was safe to move, they commenced to crawl along the outside of the wire, trying by the sense of touch to find out what havoc had been made in it by the American artillery fire and where it would be easiest to break through.

They had drawn on rubber gloves, for they knew that the

Germans sometimes charged the wires with electricity, and a touch with the bare hand would mean instant death.

But that day the fighting had been so fierce and the enemy had been kept so busy in resisting the American onslaught that no such precaution had been taken. And this better than anything else told the boys how badly the enemy had been shaken.

At several places they found gaps that had been made by the Yankee guns, and these they widened by the use of the wire cutters that they carried in their belts.

At each such breach the boys tied small pieces of white rag, so that on the next day these fluttering bits of white could be seen through field glasses by the American officers, and the full force of guns and men could be brought to bear against these weakened portions of the line.

They worked rapidly and silently, timing their cutting with the roar of the guns that still kept up the artillery duel, so that the click of the nippers would be drowned in the heavier sound.

Little by little in the course of the work, the members of the patrol had drawn apart, depending upon their ability to rejoin each other by following the line of the wire.

Frank found himself working on a specially tangled bit of wire that was made still more difficult of handling because it was intertwisted with the stalks of a thick hedge. He had just nipped a piece of wire in two, when his quick ear detected a sound on the other side of the hedge.

Instantly he stiffened. Every muscle became as taut as tempered steel. He scarcely seemed to breathe while his unwinking eyes tried to bore through the mass of tangled brush and wire to see what was on the other side.

There too the rustling sound had ceased and a silence prevailed as deep as his own.

For minutes that seemed ages this condition persisted. Then slowly, so slowly that Frank at first was not sure that he saw aright, a slender spear-like point broke the outline of the top of the hedge. Only the fact that it stood out against the dim light that came from the enemy trench enabled Frank to see it at all.

Gradually the object rose higher until it seemed to broaden out at the base; and then with a quickening of the pulse Frank realized that what he saw was the spike of a German helmet!

He had won in the duel of silence. The other, unable to stand the strain, had risen first. Would he win in the grimmer duel that seemed to be impending?

Frank's fingers stole toward his revolver, but stopped before they reached it. There must be no shooting so near the enemy trench. A horde of Germans would be upon him in a twinkling.

His rifle lay beside him where he had placed it while working on the wire. His fingers closed upon the stock. Here was a weapon that he might use at either end with deadly effect. The butt could serve as a club, while the bayonet, painted black like the rest of his accoutrements so that no glimmer of steel should betray it, carried death on its point.

Now beneath the helmet the head of a man appeared, then the shoulders, and finally the sentry, evidently satisfied that his suspicion had been without foundation, straightened out to his full length. He stood for another minute or two peering into the darkness. But Frank's black-clad form merged so perfectly into its surroundings and he remained so motionless that the German at last was convinced.

With a grunt of satisfaction he stooped to pick up his rifle.

Lithe as a panther, Frank sprang to his feet, leaped over the hedge and landed heavily on the stooping form, knocking the breath out of the German's body.

In a flash Frank's sinewy hands were upon the sentry's throat, stifling the cry that sought to issue from his lips.

There was a brief struggle, but the attack had been so sudden and tremendous that it was soon over, and the German lay limp and unconscious.

The instant Frank realized this, he relaxed his hold. He tore open the man's coat, felt for his heart and found that it was still beating.

What his foe would have done if the case had been reversed, Frank knew perfectly well. A dagger point would have pierced his heart and stilled its beating forever. More than once he had looked on the bodies of comrades who had been butchered while lying wounded and helpless on the battlefield, and had been stirred by a wild desire to take similar vengeance on those who had violated all the laws of war.

But he was an American, with all the proud traditions of honor and chivalry that had come down to him through generations. He could not slaughter a helpless foe. He had the man a prisoner. It was enough.

Quickly he tied the sentry's hands, using the German's own belt as a strap. Then he tore some strips from the white cloth he had been carrying to fasten on the bushes and made a gag, in case the man should recover his senses and try to give the alarm.

He dragged the man through a gap in the hedge so that he would not be found by any of his comrades who might come that way. Then he crept down to where the corporal and the other members of the patrol were still busy on the wires and in a whisper told what had happened.

Wilson was quick to see the opportunity that the capture had afforded.

"Good work, Sheldon," he commended. "Here's where we get through the wires. And we've got to do it quickly, for we don't know at what time that fellow's relief may be coming along."

His prophecy seemed about to be fulfilled with startling suddenness, for, even while he spoke, a group of several figures, topped by helmets, was revealed by the action of one of them in striking a match. It flared up brightly for a second, but luckily the boys were outside the zone of light that it formed.

They lay perfectly still, although each of them took a tighter grasp on his rifle.

The men conversed in guttural tones for several minutes, that seemed as many ages to the watchers in the shadows.

Would the Germans come toward them or walk away from them? Their lives, or at the least their liberty, might depend upon the answer.

One of the men pointed in their direction and even took a step forward, but his comrades stopped him and an animated discussion ensued, which finally resulted in their retracing their steps in the direction from which they had come.

A sigh of relief went up from the boys and their grip on their weapons relaxed.

"A mighty close shave," whispered Billy.

"It was all of that," agreed Bart.

"As close for them as it was for us," said Tom grimly. "I had that big fellow picked out and I'd have dropped him sure."

Like so many ghosts, the party drifted along in Corporal Wilson's wake until they came to the gap. A glance at the motionless sentry showed that he had not yet returned to consciousness.

"That was a knockout for fair," murmured Billy admiringly.

"He must have thought a house was falling on him," whispered Bart with a low chuckle.

"Frank's no featherweight," agreed Tom. "I'd hate to have those trench clogs of his come down on my back with him inside of them."

A warning "s—sh" from the corporal brought them back to the grim business still before them, and they crept along behind him as he wormed his way through the breach.

Camp utensils were scattered upon the ground and indicated that a field kitchen had stood there recently, an impression that became a conviction when Bart burned his hand by bringing it down upon some smoldering embers covered with ashes.

He bit his tongue trying to repress the exclamation that leaped to his lips, but he succeeded, although his fingers were badly blistered.

Little by little, with many pauses, they reached the edge of a small section of the first trench. Nothing hindered them, no one challenged them. In fact their progress was so free from obstacles that the corporal, a wily veteran who had had long experience among the savage Moros while serving in the Philippines, became uneasy, fearing an ambush.

Still, that was one of the chances that the party had to take, and there was nothing to do but to keep on. But they redoubled their precautions, every sense tingling with watchfulness against a sudden surprise.

They worked their way along the trench until they reached the entrance. No sound came from the interior. They listened for the murmur of conversation, the scraping of feet, the clank of a weapon. They looked down its length for a ray of light. Not a gleam or a sound rewarded them.

As far as they could judge, it was absolutely deserted. But on the other hand it might be bristling with armed men, waiting in a stillness as deathlike as their own the command to fire.

For fully ten minutes their watch continued. Then the corporal gathered them close around him and gave his commands in a whisper.

"We'll raid it," he decided. "There are only a few of us, but we'll have the advantage of surprise. That is, if they're not waiting to surprise us. But we'll have to gamble on that. It's only a connecting trench, and there won't be more than a dozen men or thereabouts in it. If we could bag them and take them back to camp it would be a good night's work. Have your guns ready and be prepared to slip them a few grenades if we have to. I'll lead the way and when the time comes I'll flash my light. Come along now and be right on your toes when I give the word."

Corporal Wilson went first and his scouting party followed close on his heels. It was like going into the jaws of death. It would have taken less nerve to face a charge, for then their blood would have been up and they would have been fired by the sight of their enemy. There would have been nothing of this eerie stillness, this vault-like chill. Yet not one of them hesitated or lagged behind.

Twenty paces had been covered when the corporal stopped, drew out his flashlight and sent out a stream of radiance that illumined every nook and cranny of the trench.

On the instant the boys had their rifles at their shoulders with their fingers on the triggers, ready for a volley.

But their precaution was needless. The trench was empty!

Empty as far as men were concerned. But it was full of other things that made their hair stand up with horror as their meaning swept in upon them!

CHAPTER VI

A TASTE OF COLD STEEL

Planted at intervals in the trench were rows of iron stakes, coming to a sharp point at the top and cunningly camouflaged so that they would not be detected by any one looking over the edge. The Army boys were not slow in seeing the meaning of the trap and the fiendish ingenuity that had conceived it.

"It's a dummy trench!" murmured Corporal Wilson. "The idea is to have their men seem to retreat into it when the fighting takes place on this part of the line. Our boys come on in pursuit, jump over the edge, come down on these sharp stakes and are spitted like larks. Nice way to wage war, that!"

"It's worthy of the Hun," growled Tom.

"And when you've said that you've reached the limit," observed Bart.

"The Turks are pretty good at torture," murmured Frank bitterly, "but they must feel like thirty cents when they compare themselves with their German masters."

"Let's get these things out of the way," said Billy wrathfully, as he grasped one of the spikes.

But the corporal stopped him instantly. "Don't dig them out!" he cried. "There's no knowing but what you may cause an explosion. Or they may have some electric connection that will give warning to the Boches. We've spotted the location of this infernal trap and that's enough. Our officers will see that our men steer clear of it."

"Of course," remarked Bart, "all the value to the Huns of this trap depends upon our boys jumping in from the top of the trench. If they came in from the entrance to the dugout, all the trouble of planting these spikes would be thrown away."

"It would be a trap just the same, only in a different way," replied the corporal. "It's a safe bet that the Germans have machine guns planted where they can sweep the whole length of this part of the trench. They'd wait until our boys were all crowded in here and then the machine guns would start spitting and wipe every last one of them out. There'd be no way to get put except the way they had come in, and no one could get through that storm of bullets. But now let's get out of this while the going's good."

The conversation had been carried on in the faintest whispers, and after the first hurried examination of the dummy trench there had been no light. But they all felt better when they had passed out of the trench without mishap and lay on the ground above. Here they were at least in the open, and if death came to them they would not be slaughtered like rats in a trap.

The corporal consulted his radio watch and found that it wanted but two hours to dawn.

"Not much time left, boys," he murmured. "And unless we get back to our lines before daylight, we'll stand a good chance of losing the number of our mess. But if we don't do anything else, we've done a pretty fair night's work. The finding of this dummy trench will put a crimp in the Heinies' plans. I'd like to have some prisoners to take along just for luck but all we've bagged is that sentry."

"Perhaps we haven't even got him," suggested Frank. "Some of his comrades may have found him by this time."

"Not likely," replied Bart. "He couldn't make a noise, and as we left him outside the wire they wouldn't be likely to stumble over him."

"All the same, we'd better get a hustle on," replied the corporal, and they started on their homeward journey as stealthily as they had come.

They had some difficulty in finding the breach in the wire through which they had entered, but at last they succeeded and wormed their way out. Then they felt around for the sentry and found him in the place they had left him. He had returned to consciousness, for when the corporal risked a ray of his flashlight on the upturned face, they could see that his eyes were open and looking at them intelligently.

The corporal placed the muzzle of his revolver against the man's neck as a gentle reminder of what would happen to him if he should make a sound, and they proceeded to untie his hands. Then they motioned to him that he was to get on his hands and knees and go before them, which, with muffled grunts, and after two or three attempts, he succeeded in doing. He was evidently dazed yet and stiff from the cramped attitude in which he had been lying, but stern necessity was on him and he finally wobbled and staggered on before them.

They had got some little distance away from the wires when Frank suddenly came to a dead stop. His comrades halted instantly.

"What is it?" whispered Wilson, who was nearest to him.

"That blur ahead of us," returned Frank. "It looks a little more solid than the rest of the darkness."

He pointed ahead and a little to the right.

"I don't see anything," remarked Tom.

"Neither do I," affirmed Billy.

"I think I see a little blacker patch than usual," declared Bart. "And it seems to be moving."

The corporal put his ear to the ground.

"I think Sheldon is right," he said, after a moment of intense listening. "At any rate we'll take no chances. Slip into some of these shell holes and lie low. If it should be an enemy patrol and there are too many to tackle we'll let them go by. But if there aren't more than double our number we'll take a crack at them. Keep your weapons ready and let fly when I give the word."

The ground was so pitted with craters from the heavy artillery duel that had been raging all the day before that they had no difficulty in finding shelter. Their prisoner, who judged by the preparations that some of his own comrades were approaching, was inclined to balk a little and delay matters, but a vigorous push of Bart's boot hastened his movements and he was tumbled in unceremoniously. And they blessed the precaution that had still left the gag in his mouth when they had unfastened his hands.

More and more the blur ahead of them detached itself from the surrounding darkness, until even skeptical Tom and Billy knew that what they saw was a body of men bearing down steadily in their direction.

Of course there was a chance that it was an American patrol out on an errand similar to their own, but it was unlikely, if that were so, that they would be going in the direction of the enemy's lines when the night was so far spent.

Nearer and nearer came the party until not more than thirty feet lay between them and the American boys who knelt in the shell holes, with faces stern and set and fingers on the triggers of their rifles awaiting the word of command.

But for some unknown reason the blur became motionless and remained so for several minutes. Then it receded, as though the party had changed its plan.

"What do you suppose is the matter with them?" whispered Tom. "Do you think they've tumbled to our being here?"

"How could they?" returned Frank. "They'd have to have the eyes of cats to see us in these holes."

"I hope the corp will let us go after them," murmured Billy. "I'm all tuned up for a scrap."

Wilson hesitated. If he went after the supposed enemy, they would probably hear him and he would lose the advantage of the surprise. On the other hand, that they now seemed to be going in the direction of the American lines might indicate that, after all, they were a patrol of his own comrades. But while he weighed the chances, the question was solved for him by the fact that the blur again became distinct. And this time it grew larger very rapidly, indicating that the party had at last reached a definite decision. On they came until only a few paces separated them from the Army boys.

Just then a star shell rose from the German lines and sent a flare of light stabbing the darkness and clearly revealing a dozen or more Germans. As they were facing the glare they were momentarily dazzled by it, and the Americans peering beneath their black hoods on a level with the ground could have easily escaped detection had they been so inclined.

But that instantaneous flash had decided the corporal. The odds were more than two to one, but such odds as that was only a challenge to Yankee fighting blood.

"Fire!" he shouted, and five rifles spoke as one. Three of the enemy went down as though stricken by an axe, and another staggered and his rifle clattered to the ground.

But the enemy rallied almost instantly, and at a hoarse command there was a return volley. This proved harmless, however, for the boys knew that it would come and bent beneath the edge of the craters until the iron storm had swept over them.

"Now, boys, at them with your bayonets!" shouted Corporal Wilson, as soon as he had drawn the enemy's fire.

With a leap the American squad was on the level ground and rushing with leveled bayonets at the foe.

The Americans had the advantage of the surprise, and their headlong charge would have won instantly if the forces had been equal. But although two went down at once, the others, after yielding ground somewhat, closed in a death grip with their assailants, and there was a furious combat at close quarters.

There was no more shooting. It was a matter now of clubbed rifles and bayonet thrusts.

Frank found himself engaged in a bayonet duel with a massive German who towered above him in height and probably outweighed him by twenty pounds. He was well trained too in bayonet work and was a most formidable opponent.

But he met his master when he crossed bayonets with Frank. The latter had made himself expert by long training under skilful French instructors, and, besides, was the most finished boxer in the regiment. At thrust and parry, feint and riposte, advance and retreat, he stood first among his comrades.

Against the furious bull-like rushes of his opponent, he opposed a quickness and agility that more than counter-balanced his enemy's weight It was a contest of a bull against a panther, and the panther won.

For perhaps two minutes the fight continued. Then with a lightning thrust Frank's bayonet found its mark, and the German staggered for a moment, fell headlong and lay still.

His fall seemed to take the heart out of the others who were being outfought and pressed back. They wavered, broke and started to flee, but the sharp crack of the corporal's revolver brought one of them to the ground, and the others halted.

Up went their hands and from the lips of each came the cry

"*Kamerad*!" in token of surrender.

The American boys rounded them up and disarmed them. Then the corporal took account of stock.

Bart was there panting and flushed with nothing worse than a scalp wound where a rifle butt had glanced from his head. Wilson himself was unhurt. Billy also had come through unscathed, but Tom was nowhere to be seen.

An awful fear, a fear that they had never felt in the fighting itself, clutched the hearts of his comrades. Good old Tom, bound to them by a thousand ties of friendship and comradeship—had he met his fate in this desolate stretch of No Man's Land?

Frantically they searched among the bodies for one that wore a suit similar to their own. Frank found it first. His hand went to the heart and to his joy found that it was beating.

He lifted Tom's head and rested it on his knee.

"Tom! Tom!" he called, as he chafed his chum's hands and loosened his suit at the throat.

Tom's eyes slowly opened, and, recognizing his friend, a faint smile came to his lips. But he did not speak, and Bart, who was the only other one who could be spared from guarding the prisoners, joined Frank in redoubled efforts to bring Tom back to full consciousness.

"He doesn't seem to have any bones broken," said Frank after a hurried examination.

"And he isn't bleeding," replied Bart. "But he has a lump on his head as big as an egg."

At last Tom's full consciousness returned, and with his chums' assistance he got slowly and painfully to his feet.

"Guess they haven't got my number yet, but they came mighty near it," he said, trying to grin. "I'd just run one of the Huns through the arm when I saw another out of the tail of my eye swinging for my head with his rifle. I tried to dodge, but he must have been too quick for me, for that's the last I remember."

"Thank heaven it was no worse!" ejaculated Frank fervently.

"It would have been a mighty bad thing for us if you had cashed in, old boy," said Bart with feeling. "How did the scrap turn out?" asked Tom.

"Though I suppose there's no use in asking, or you wouldn't be here taking care of me."

"We trimmed them good and proper," said Frank, from whom a ton's weight had been lifted by finding that his friend had escaped serious injury.

"A lovely scrap," added Bart. "I wouldn't have missed it for a farm. We've wiped out five and rounded out the rest. Let's go over and see how many there are."

"Eight," announced the corporal, as he counted the prisoners who stood in a group sullen and morose. "There must have been a baker's dozen in the party."

"I don't know how superstitious they may be," chuckled Billy, "but I'll bet that from now on they'll agree that thirteen is an unlucky number!"

CHAPTER VII

NICK RABIG'S QUEER ACTIONS

"Well," remarked Corporal Wilson, who was relieved beyond measure to find that his own little force was practically intact, "eight is a pretty good bag for one night's work, not to speak of five more who won't do any more strafing for the Kaiser."

"Nine," corrected Bart. "Don't forget our speechless friend in the shell hole."

"No doubt he'd be perfectly willing to be forgotten," grinned Billy. "But we'd better take him along just for luck. That'll be nearly two prisoners apiece for each of the bunch. Pretty fair work if you ask me."

There was no further time for talking, for it would soon be dawn and they were eager to get back to their own lines. They had been under a terrible strain through all the long hours of the night and were beginning to feel the reaction. And they were not at all averse to showing their comrades in the regiment how well they had fared and how stoutly they had held up the colors of the old Thirty-seventh.

"Who goes there?" came the sharp challenge of the sentry, as they drew near the American trench, and they knew that a score of rifles was trained upon them to back up the sentry's demand if the answer were halting or suspicious.

"Friends," replied the corporal.

"Advance and give the countersign," was the next requirement.

Corporal Wilson complied, and he and his squad were joyfully welcomed.

"I said 'friends'" added the corporal with a grin, as the party made their way through the opening in the wire defences, "but perhaps that doesn't go for all this crowd. Some of them didn't want to come, but we told them they'd better, and here they are."

"A bunch of huskies," remarked the sentry, as he surveyed the prisoners critically. "You don't mean to say that just you five rounded up that gang?"

The four privates merely grinned.

"Looks like it, doesn't it?" answered the corporal with keen relish of the sentry's surprise. "Counting those we brought down, there are just fourteen that will turn up missing when the Boches call the roll this morning."

"That's going some," said the sentry admiringly. "I only wish I'd been along with you. Some fellows have all the luck."

The prisoners were turned over to the officer in charge, and the corporal made his way to headquarters to make his report of the night's work.

Bart and Tom went under the hands of the surgeons to have their wounds and bruises treated, and were assured that with a little rest they would be as well as ever in a day or two. Then the boys, "dog-tired," as Bart expressed it, but happy and exultant that they had done their work well and were back safe once more, tumbled into their bunks to enjoy the rest they had so richly earned.

"Never was so tired in my life," murmured Frank, drowsily, as he fell rather than climbed into his bunk.

"Same here," chimed in Billy.

"Rip Van Winkle won't have anything on me," drawled Tom. "What's twenty years of sleep? I'm going to take forty."

As for Bart, he started to say something but dropped off to sleep while saying it.

None of the quartette woke until late in the afternoon. Then they found that their exploit had made a stir in the regiment. Their fight against twice their number was the most interesting feature to their comrades of the rank and file. But still more important in the view of their officers was the discovery of the dummy trench, which might have been turned into a shambles for the American troops if they had rushed into the trap so cunningly and so fiendishly set for them.

"It was fine work, Corporal," the captain said warmly, when Wilson finished his report. "You deserve credit for having brought your squad back without the loss of a man."

"They mostly brought themselves back, sir," replied Wilson with a smile. "It's a pleasure to command such a nervy crowd as that. You don't need to use the spur. I'm mostly busy putting on the brakes. It would have done your heart good if you could have seen the way they waded into the Huns. That fellow Sheldon particularly is a crackerjack when it comes to a scrap. He's as strong as an ox and as quick as a cat."

"I've had my eye on him," replied the officer. "He'll go far before the war is over. You can go now, Corporal. I'll have your work mentioned in the order of the day."

He was as good as his word, for when the regiment was drawn up for inspection the order of the day commended each man of the squad by name for their gallant exploit that, as the order ran, "reflected credit on the regiment."

"How's your head feeling now, old man?" Frank asked of Tom, as they rejoined each other at mess.

"Pretty groggy," responded Tom. "But I'm not kicking. I'm lucky to be alive at all. That fellow made an awful swipe at me, and if it had hit me fair it would have been all over."

"A miss is as good as a mile," put in Bart. "I had a pretty close shave myself. Seemed as though twenty star shells were going off at once."

"Yesterday was your lucky day," remarked Billy. "You had two narrow escapes."

"Let's hope it won't be three times and out," responded Bart lightly." By the way, I wonder what they did with that corporal who tried to do me up?"

"Most likely he's shot by this time," observed Tom. "If he isn't, he ought to be."

"He isn't shot yet at any rate," remarked Fred Andon, who sat near by. "I guess the fighting was so hot all day yesterday that they didn't have time to attend to him. Likely enough he's down in the prisoners' pen waiting for the court-martial."

"Let's go down and see after we've finished our chow," suggested Billy. "That is if you fellows ever get through eating. Look at Tom stowing it away. He'd eat his way through the whole quartermaster's department if he was let."

"And he's the fellow that they wouldn't let enlist because of his teeth," gibed Bart. "They didn't know Tom."

"I'm not the only one that got a raw deal," replied Tom, with whom it was always a sore point that he had been refused when he wanted to enlist, but had been accepted in the draft. "There's a drafted man here who was telling me the other day that he walked ninety miles to enlist. And do you know what the enlistment board did to him?"

"What?" was the query.

"Turned him down because he had flat feet," responded Tom. "Told him he wouldn't be able to stand a five-mile hike."

There was a roar of laughter.

"I heard another good one," chimed in Billy. "A fellow wanted to enlist, and the examining board wanted to reject him because he had a cast in his eye. 'Oh, that's all right,' he drawled, 'I allus shets that eye anyway when I shoot.' That made them laugh and he got by."

In high spirits they finished their meal, and as they were off duty for the next hour or two, made their way down to that quarter of the field where the prisoners' camp was placed.

Behind the barrier at the point nearest them they saw one bulky captive, who was munching contentedly the food that had been given him, and who had none of the woe-begone expression that a man in his position is commonly expected to show.

"See him shovel it in," laughed Billy.

"He doesn't seem to have a care in the world," remarked Bart.

"Probably glad to be behind our machine guns instead of in front of them," conjectured Tom.

"Hello, Heinie!" said Frank good-naturedly.

"Hello yourself," came the answer.

"Do you speak English?" asked Frank in surprise.

"A little," replied the German, and proceeded to prove it by answering, although in rather a halting manner, the questions they put to him.

No, he at any rate had not wanted the war. He was a skilled mechanic in one of the munition factories. There had been a strike on account of bad conditions and he had been one of the leaders. The Government had seized him and bundled him off to the front. He was glad to be captured. After the war the Kaiser would see that men were born to be something else than cannon fodder.

"Well," remarked Frank as they moved along, "there's one fellow at least that doesn't cry: '*Hoch the Kaiser*.'"

"Seems good to see it so full," remarked Bart with great

satisfaction, as he saw the large number of Germans who had been captured in the fierce fighting of the day before.

"If only the Kaiser and the Crown Prince were in that bunch," sighed Tom.

"That's a pleasure still to come," replied Frank. "But where's the fellow that tried to stab Bart? I don't see him anywhere. Seems as though the party isn't complete without him."

They made inquiry of one of the guards.

"Oh, that one," replied the guard. "They've roped him out from the rest of these mavericks and given him a hut all by himself. I guess he's thinking of making his will. I hear they're going to have him out before a drumhead in the morning."

"Which hut is it?" asked Frank, as his eye took in a little group of shacks at the further end of the field.

"That end one down by the big tree." The guard pointed it out with the point of his bayonet.

They went down in that direction, and as they neared the hut saw that it was guarded by a single sentry.

"Who's that fellow on guard?" asked Tom. "My head's so dizzy yet that I'm seeing things double."

"Looks rather familiar for a fact," said Bart. "Wait till he turns his head this way."

The next instant the sentry turned, and there was a whistle of surprise from Billy. "By the great horn spoon!" he ejaculated. "It's Nick Rabig!"

"Set a Hun to watch a Hun," remarked Tom bitingly.

"Oh, come, Tom," remonstrated Frank, "that's going a little too far. I've no reason to like the fellow, and we know he had to be dragged into the army, but that doesn't say he's a Hun."

"All except the uniform," persisted Tom. "He'd rather be fighting for the Kaiser this minute than for Uncle Sam."

"Shouldn't wonder if Tom's more than half right," assented Billy. "You know the way he" used to talk in Camport."

"You notice that we've never seen him volunteering for any of the raiding parties," said Billy.

"But that may only mean that Rabig has a yellow streak in him. It doesn't say that he's a traitor," returned Frank.

"Well, maybe he isn't," conceded Tom. "But all the same it seems rather queer that he should have been picked out to guard this Heinie. They could talk together in German through that closed door and nobody be wise to what they were saying."

"I don't suppose the officers know Rabig as well as the rest of us do," said Billy. "But say, fellows, look at that bit of white under the door of the hut. What do you suppose it is?"

"Oh, just a scrap of paper," laughed Bart. "Just like the Belgian treaty."

"Something the wind's blown up against the door, I guess," conjectured Tom.

"Wind nothing!" exclaimed Frank, whose vision was keener than that of any of the others. "It's under the door and it's getting bigger and bigger all the time. I tell you what it is, fellows," he went on excitedly, "it's a note that's being pushed out by the fellow inside."

"Let's get behind these trees and see what's going on," suggested Bart, indicating a clump of trees near which they happened to be standing.

In a moment they were screened from observation. Then they watched with the keenest interest what would follow.

That Rabig had caught sight of the paper was evident, for he stopped his pacing and turned his eyes on the door. Then he looked stealthily about him. The nearest sentry was some distance away, and the boys were well hidden by the trees.

Then Rabig made a complete circuit of the little hut, as though to make sure that no one was lurking about. Having apparently satisfied himself on that point, he returned and resumed his pacing until he was directly in front of the door.

Here he paused and drew out his handkerchief and wiped his forehead. But as he went to put it back, it dropped from his hand so that it lay close by and almost upon the protruding piece of paper.

He was stooping to pick it up, when he caught sight of a sergeant coming in his direction. Instantly he straightened up, and as he did so the butt of his rifle knocked against the door.

The paper disappeared as though it had been drawn swiftly back from the inside, just as the sergeant came up.

"Gee!" gasped Tom.

"Prisoner all right, Rabig?" inquired the sergeant.

"Yes, sir," replied Rabig. "He seems to be keeping pretty quiet. I looked in a little while ago and he was lying asleep on the bench."

"Keep a close watch on him," counseled the sergeant. "What he tried to do to Raymond yesterday shows that he's a desperate character. But I guess that by this time to-morrow he won't need any one to watch him."

The sergeant passed on and the boys looked at each other with speculation in their eyes.

"What do you think of it?" asked Frank thoughtfully.

"Think?" snorted Tom. "I think that Rabig is a bad egg. What else is there for any one to think?"

"It certainly looks suspicious," said Bart with a little wrinkle of anxiety creasing his brow.

"One thing is sure," declared Billy. "It was a note that was being pushed outside that door. The fellow inside was trying to get into communication with Rabig."

"True," assented Frank. "But that in itself doesn't prove anything. You or I might be on sentry duty and a prisoner might try to do the same thing to us."

"Yes," agreed Billy. "But we wouldn't act the way Rabig did. We'd have picked up the note and given it to the sergeant of the guard."

"And we wouldn't have sneaked around the hut to see if any one was near by," said Tom. "Why did he drop his handkerchief, except to have an excuse for picking it up and copping the note at the same time?"

"And his rifle butt didn't hit the door by accident," put in Billy. "That was a tip to the prisoner that some one was coming. Did you see how quickly the note disappeared?"

"I hate to think that there's a single man in the regiment who's a disgrace to his uniform," remarked Frank, "but it certainly looks bad. That fellow Rabig will bear watching."

"I told you he was a Hun," declared Tom. "His body's in France, but his heart's in Germany."

CHAPTER VIII

COLONEL PAVET REAPPEARS

The Army boys thought over the situation in some perplexity.

"What do you suppose we ought to do?" asked Bart.

"We ought to go hotfoot to the captain and tell him what we've seen," declared Tom with emphasis.

"I hardly like to do that," objected Billy. "At least not at this stage of the game. After all, we haven't any positive proof against Nick. His handkerchief might have dropped accidentally. And the knocking of the butt of his gun against the door could have happened without his meaning anything by it. He could explain his going around the hut by saying he wanted to be especially vigilant in guarding the prisoner."

"Yes," agreed Frank, "we haven't proof enough against Rabig to hang a yellow dog. And I wouldn't want to get him in bad with his officers on mere suspicion."

"That note might be proof if we could only get hold of it," suggested Tom.

"Swell chance!" returned Bart. "You can bet that note is chewed up and swallowed by this time. The first thing the Hun thought of, when he was tipped off that some one was coming, was to get rid of the evidence that might queer his chance of escape."

"I'll tell you what we'll do," said Frank. "We'll just go down and see Rabig and ask him casually about the prisoner. That may make him think that we're on to something, and if he's planning to do anything crooked it may scare him off. It won't do any harm anyway, and we'll take a chance."

They left the clump of trees and strolled down carelessly in the direction of the hut.

Rabig saw them coming, and the surly look that was habitual with him became more pronounced than usual. There was no love lost between him and any of them. He had been thoroughly unpopular in Camport because of his bullying nature even before the outbreak of the war, and his evident leaning toward Germany had deepened this feeling.

Since he had been drafted, he had of course kept his pro-German views to himself, for he valued his skin and had no desire to face a firing squad. But his work had been done grudgingly, and his disposition to shirk had more than once gained him short terms in the guardhouse.

Of all the group approaching him he most heartily disliked Frank. In the first place, Frank had never permitted him to bully him when they were with Moore & Thomas, and the two had been more than once on the brink of a fight. And since the boxing bout in the camp, when he had tried foul tactics and Frank had thrashed him thoroughly, his venom toward his conqueror had been more bitter than ever.

The boys stopped when they reached the front of the hut.

"Hello, Rabig!" they greeted him.

"Hello!" responded Rabig, still keeping up his pacing.

"Right on the job, I see," remarked Bart, pleasantly enough.

"Your eyesight's mighty good," replied Nick sullenly.

"Yes," Bart came back at him, "I can see a bit of white paper from quite a distance."

Rabig gave a sudden start.

"What do you mean by that?" he demanded.

"Nothing special," replied Bart carelessly. "What should I mean?"

"By the way," put in Tom, "you'd better tuck your handkerchief in a little more tightly or you'll lose it. It looks as though it were almost ready to drop out."

"What if it does?" snarled Rabig. "I could pick it up again, couldn't I?"

"Of course you could," said Tom, "but you might pick up something else with it. Dust, or a bit of paper, or something like that."

"Say, what's the matter with you guys anyway?" demanded Rabig, glowering at them.

"That looks like quite a solid door," remarked Frank, inspecting it critically.

"Oh, I don't know," responded Billy. "It's got dents in it. Here's one that looks as though it were made by a rifle butt."

Rabig looked at them angrily, and yet furtively, evidently seeking to find out how much their remarks meant.

"You fellows had better get along," he snapped. "You're interfering with discipline by talking to a sentry on guard."

Rabig's newborn reverence for discipline amused the boys so that they had hard work to repress a laugh.

"You're right," responded Frank. "We'll mosey along."

"Ta-ta, Rabig," said Bart. "Keep your eye peeled for any Hun trick. That fellow nearly got me yesterday with his knife, and he might try to play the same game on you."

"Don't you worry," growled Rabig. "I can take care of myself."

The chums passed on, laughing and talking about indifferent things, until they were out of ear shot.

"We've got him guessing," remarked Billy with a grin.

"We managed to put a flea in his ear," agreed Tom.

"Did you see how red he got?" questioned Bart.

"He sure is wondering how much we know," summed up Frank. "Whether it will make him go straight or not is another question. What we fellows ought to do is to take turns keeping tab on him, so that he can't act crooked even if he wants to." "It's a pity there should be any men in the American army whom we have to watch," said Tom bitterly.

"Yes, but that's to be expected," returned Frank. "There's never been an army in the history of the world that hasn't been infected with traitors more or less."

"Look at Benedict Arnold," remarked Billy.

"To my mind, it's surprising that there aren't more," said Frank. "That's what the Kaiser was counting on. He thought that the German element in America was so strong that we wouldn't dare to go to war with him. Do you remember what he told Gerard? That 'there were five hundred thousand Germans in America who would revolt'?"

"Yes," grinned Billy, "and I remember how Gerard came back at him with the 'five hundred thousand lamp-posts on which we'd hang them if they did.'"

They were out on the main road by this time, and they stepped to one side and saluted, as an officer in French uniform, accompanied by an orderly, came galloping along.

The officer's eye swept the group as he returned the salute, and when it rested on Frank he drew up his horse so suddenly that the beast sat back on its haunches.

The officer threw himself from the horse's back, cast the reins to his orderly, and came impetuously toward the astonished Army boys with his hand extended to Frank.

"Monsieur Sheldon!" he exclaimed, his face beaming. "*Mon brave Americain. Le sauveur de ma vie.*"

"Colonel Pavet!" cried Frank with equal pleasure, as he took the extended hand.

"Yes," replied the newcomer, "Colonel Pavet, alive and well, thanks to you. Ah, I shall never forget the night when I lay wounded on the battlefield and you climbed out of the trench and made your way through a storm of bullets and shells to my side and carried me back to safety. It was the deed of a hero, a modern d'Artagnan! How glad I am to see you again!"

"And I to see you" responded Frank warmly. "You were so dreadfully wounded that I feared you might not recover."

They were talking in French, which Frank spoke like a native, thanks to his French mother, and the other boys saluted and passed on, leaving the two together.

"If we had not met, I would have searched you out," went on the colonel, "for I have some news for you. News that both you and your mother will be glad to hear."

"My mother," repeated Frank, his eyes kindling and his heart responding, as it never failed to do at the mention of that dear mother of his, who in her lonely home across the sea was waiting and praying for him.

CHAPTER IX

THE ESCAPE

"Yes," replied Colonel Pavet, "your mother, Madame Sheldon,—it seems strange for me to name her thus, for I never think of her except as Lucie De Latour, as I knew her in her girlhood—has a very excellent prospect of coming into the property that was willed to her."

"I'm very glad to hear that!" exclaimed Frank. "And I know that my mother will be pleased too. I have told her in my letters about my meeting with you, and I gave her the remembrances that you were kind enough to send her. She was delighted to know that I had met one of her old neighbors in Auvergne, and she asked me to thank you most heartily for your kindness in promising to look after her interests."

The colonel smiled genially.

"She is too good," he responded. "The obligation is all on my side. My humble services would have been at her disposal in any event simply for the sake of old friendship. But how much more ought they to be wholly hers, now that her son has saved my life."

"I am afraid you put too much value on what I did, Colonel," said Frank deprecatingly.

"It was something that not one in ten thousand would have done," replied the colonel warmly. "When I found myself helpless and wounded on that field of death I thought my life was over, and I had commended my soul to God."

"I'm glad that you have lived to strike another blow for France," said Frank.

"Ah, for France!" repeated the colonel fervently, as he lifted his cap reverently.

"As I started to say," he resumed after a moment, "your mother's prospects for coming into her own are excellent. After my wound I was sent home, and for some time it was doubtful whether I would live or die. But God was good and I recovered. While I was gradually mending I had ample time to look into that matter of the contested will. And, fortunately, just at that time my brother Andre, who is one of the leading lawyers of Paris, came to the chateau to see and cheer me up while I was convalescing. I laid the whole matter before him, and he went into it thoroughly. He has gone over all the proceedings in the case, and he tells me that there is no doubt that your mother has the law as well as right—unfortunately they are not always the same thing—on her side. He says that the testimony of those who are contesting the will smacks strongly of perjury. It is too bad that your mother cannot be here, for then Andre thinks the whole thing could be straightened out at once."

"It is too bad," agreed Frank; "but in the present state of things, and the danger on the Atlantic from submarines, I would not want her to take the risk. But what you say delights me, as I am sure it will her, and I can't thank you enough for all the trouble you have taken."

"Not trouble, but pleasure," corrected the colonel. "And you can be assured that the matter will not be allowed to lag now that Andre has taken it up. When he starts a case he can be depended on to carry it through to a finish. I will keep in close touch with him and will let you know from time to time how the matter is progressing. But now tell me about yourself."

"There's not much to tell," replied Frank. "I'm well and have been lucky enough so far not to have stopped a bullet."

The colonel's eyes twinkled.

"Not much to tell," he repeated. "No, not if Monsieur Sheldon does the telling. But there are others who speak more freely. Your captain, for instance."

Frank flushed uncomfortably and Colonel Pavet laughed outright.

"Bravery and modesty usually go together," he went on. "How about that machine gun episode yesterday, when an American soldier cut down its crew, turned it on the enemy trench and compelled the men in it to surrender? How about the raiding party where five men accounted for fourteen of the Huns? You see, *mon ami*, that I have a good memory for details. Ah, you are blushing. I wonder if you, too, could recall these things if you tried."

"There were a lot of us in on them," parried Frank, "and one did as much as another."

"Well," rejoined the colonel, "I'm proud that a French woman is your mother. You have a glorious heritage in the traditions of two gallant countries. And I rejoice to see the way you Americans are throwing yourselves into the fighting. We were sorely pressed by the Hun hordes and were fighting with our backs against the wall."

"And such fighting!" returned Frank enthusiastically. "The world has never seen anything finer. The spirit of France is unconquerable."

"Yes," replied the colonel proudly. "As one of our great orators has said: 'If the men are all killed the women will rise up; if the women are killed the children will rise; if the children are killed the very dead will rise and fight—fight for France."

"But I must go on," he continued, motioning to his orderly to bring up his horse. "I have a long journey yet before I reach the headquarters of my division. I am more delighted than I can tell that I met you as I did. May we meet again soon."

"In Berlin, if not sooner," interjected Frank with a smile.

"Ah, that is it," said the colonel delightedly. "In Berlin! That is the way to speak. It may be a long time, but sooner or later the Stars and Stripes and the Tricolor will wave together *Unter den Linden*. May Heaven speed the day!"

The French officer wrung Frank's hand warmly, sprang into the saddle, and with Frank's "*bon voyage*" ringing in his ears, galloped rapidly away.

Twilight was coming on as Frank set out to rejoin his comrades, who were waiting for him at a little distance down the road. His heart was light, for he had news to write his mother that he knew would bring her pleasure.

"Some swell," chaffed Tom, as Frank came up to his friends. "Talking to a colonel as though he were a pal. I wonder that you condescend to talk to us common privates."

"It is a comedown," grinned Frank; "but I'll try to tolerate you for a while longer. But say, fellows, that colonel is a brick! Not a bit of side about him. And he's doing a lot for us in the matter of my mother's property that I've told you about."

"That's bully!" exclaimed Bart heartily.

"I'll forgive him," conceded Tom magnanimously, "even if he does talk in a lingo that I can't understand."

"Why, I thought you were a finished French scholar by this time," chaffed Bart.

"Do you remember the day Tom tried to ask for soup and got his tongue twisted around 'bouillon'?" gibed Billy, with a broad grin.

"Well, I got the soup anyway, didn't I?" defended Tom.

"Sure you got it," agreed Billy. "I could hear you getting it."

Tom made a pass at him that Billy ducked.

"Talking about soup makes me hungry," remarked Bart. "If you fellows stand talking here much longer we'll be late at chow."

"I'd like to have one more look at that hut Rabig's guarding," said Frank a little uneasily.

"We might stroll down this way again after supper if you

like," suggested Billy, "but just at present a little knife and fork exercise seems the most pressing business I have to attend to."

Just then their talk was interrupted by a single shot, followed by a volley of them, and looking back in the direction from which they had come, they saw men running in the direction of the hut that Rabig had been guarding.

They turned and ran at full speed and were soon in the midst of an excited group gathered about the hut.

"What's up?" asked Frank of one of the soldiers.

"Prisoner escaped," replied the other briefly.

"What prisoner?"

"The fellow that Rabig was guarding. Some way or other he got out, managed to strike Rabig down and skipped. Poor Rabig's pretty badly messed up."

The boys looked at each other.

"*Poor* Rabig," repeated Tom, and there was a world of meaning in his tone.

CHAPTER X

A GHASTLY BURDEN

The sergeant of the guard came running up quickly, followed by two other officers of higher rank, and a hurried inquiry took place on the spot.

Rabig had been lifted to his feet from where he had been lying, and stood supported by two comrades. Blood was running down his face from a wound in his head. He seemed weak and dazed, although a surgeon who had been hastily summoned pronounced the wound not dangerous. He seemed to have been dealt a glancing blow, and, as in the case of all scalp wounds, the blood had flowed freely.

"Bring a seat for him," commanded the lieutenant in charge, and the order was promptly obeyed.

"Now, Rabig," proceeded the officer, not unkindly, "tell me about this. How did you come to lose your prisoner?"

Rabig looked about him in a helpless sort of way.

"I don't know," he mumbled. "My head is swimming so that I can't remember."

"Try to think," said the officer patiently. Rabig seemed to make an effort, but did not succeed and fell back in a swoon that put an end for the present to the questioning.

"Who saw anything of this?" queried the lieutenant, looking about him. "Does any one know in what direction the prisoner went?"

"If you please, sir," said one of the sentries who had been guarding an adjacent hut, "I saw a man jump on a horse and go through the woods there, but it was getting dark and I didn't know but what it might be one of our own men. But I ran up here and found Rabig lying on the ground, and the door of the hut was open. I sent a shot after the man on horseback and so did some of the other men, but we couldn't take aim and I don't know whether we hit him or not."

"Look alive there," commanded the officer. "Sergeant, take a squad of men and beat up these woods. The fellow may be hiding there. Take him dead or alive."

"Yes, sir," replied the sergeant, saluting.

The soldiers standing by were hastily sent into the woods and others were summoned to join them. The prisoner had got a good start, but by this time the field telephones were busy all along the line and his chance of ultimate escape was by no means bright. But he was a powerful and desperate man, and if he had any weapons at all he would probably make his capture a costly one.

"He'll reason that he's a dead man if we get him and he might as well die fighting," remarked Frank, as with his comrades he picked his way through the woods.

"Righto," agreed Tom. "And even if he didn't have a weapon

when he escaped, there are lots of them lying around and he won't have any trouble in picking one up."

"I wonder if he'll stick to the horse," mused Bart.

"I hardly think so," replied Billy. "He knows from the shots that were sent after him that we know he used a horse in escaping and will be looking for a man on horseback. So he'll try to deceive us by going on foot."

"He'll probably hang about in the woods until it's pitch dark and then try to get through the lines," said Frank. "He may be behind any tree or bush, and we want to be mighty careful to examine each one as we go past it."

"Maybe he'll climb a tree," suggested Tom, looking up to the branches of one he happened to be under at the moment.

"Not a chance at this time of the year," objected Billy. "There aren't any leaves to hide him, and even in the darkness we could probably see his outline against the sky. Then, too, if he were seen he could be potted too easily. No, he's not up a tree."

"Queer that he should have got away so soon after we'd been down to the hut," remarked Frank.

"Queer!" snorted Tom. "It isn't queer at all to my way of thinking. The whole thing was cut and dried."

"Then you think that Rabig was in cahoots with him?" asked Bart dubiously.

"I'm sure of it," responded Tom. "Use your common sense, fellows. We see half a dozen suspicious things that look as if Rabig and the prisoner had some understanding. A little while after the prisoner escapes. What's the answer?"

"The answer might be several things," replied Frank, who hated to believe evil of even his worst enemy. "A lot of things are due to coincidence. It may be perfectly true that Rabig was in sympathy with the German, but that doesn't say that he'd go so far as to let him actually escape. He was taking big chances with his own skin in doing it."

"Besides, there's no doubt that Rabig was wounded," remarked Bart. "That fellow seems to have given him an awful knock. He was bleeding like fury."

"Oh, it was easy enough to arrange that," answered Tom, unconvinced. "It would have been too raw to have Rabig let the fellow go and still be safe and sound. How could he explain it? He'd be brought up for court-martial. But a scalp wound could be easily made where it would produce the most blood and do the least harm."

"But what object would Rabig have in taking such chances?" asked Billy. "The fellow had been searched and couldn't have had any money with him."

"No, but he could have promised plenty," argued Tom. "Perhaps he's told Rabig that the grateful Kaiser would make him rich. How do we know that Rabig wouldn't fall for that? He's got an ivory dome anyway. If there were more than two ideas in his head at one time they'd be arrested for unlawful assemblage."

The boys laughed and Tom went on:

"Besides, how do we know but what Rabig is planning to desert and wants to pave the way for a warm welcome on the other side? It would be easy enough to slip across while the lines are so near each other."

"But Rabig seemed to be pretty badly hurt," said Billy. "You saw him faint."

"Which only proves that he is a good actor," retorted Tom dryly. "Don't think me hardhearted, fellows, because I'm not. I'm always ready to give everybody his due. But I feel sure down in my heart that this thing was all fixed up beforehand, and some day you'll find that I'm right."

For more than two hours they kept up the search without result, and the fact that they had not had their supper was forced upon them with growing insistency.

"Isn't there any time limit to this?" grumbled Bart. "I'll be hunting for acorns instead of a prisoner before long."

"I've got a vacuum where my stomach ought to be," moaned Billy. "Gee, wouldn't I like to be streaking it for the mess room."

"Cork up, you fellows," commanded Frank. "Listen! I thought I heard something just then."

The talking ceased instantly, and all stood as rigid as statues.

"It's a horse coming this way," whispered Frank, after a moment of strained attention. "Quick, fellows, get behind these bushes and have your rifles ready!"

They crouched low and peered up a little glade that ran through the forest.

But the noise ceased as suddenly as it had begun and they began to think that their comrade had been mistaken.

"Guess Frank's been stringing us," chaffed Billy.

"He's the only one who seems to have heard anything," said Tom.

"Don't you worry about my hearing," said Frank. "I tell you I heard a horse's hoofs. Perhaps the rider suspects something and is trying to get a line on us, just as we're trying to get one on him."

"It may have been a horse all right," said Billy, "but that doesn't say he had any rider. He may be rambling around all by his lonesome, and perhaps he's stopped to graze somewhere."

"There he goes again!" exclaimed Frank, and this time every one of them heard what was undeniably the thud of a horse's hoofs.

But there was a hesitation, an uncertainty about the animal's movements that seemed unusual. It moved as though it had no purpose in view no guiding hand on the reins. At times the canter seemed to subside into a walk. There was something about this unseen steed, at large in the dim forest, that gave the boys a most uncomfortable feeling.

Then suddenly a more resolute note in the sound and an increase in its volume told the listening boys that the horse was coming straight toward them.

The clatter of hoofs drew nearer, and they clutched their guns more tightly.

Soon they were able to distinguish in the gloom the outline of a horse and rider. The man's figure loomed up huge and threatening, and they felt sure that it was the big German corporal for whom they were searching.

The boys waited until the horse was almost upon them and then rushed out into the road.

"Halt!" cried Frank. He seized the horse's rein while the others leveled their rifles at the rider.

The horse reared in fright, but the rider made no answer nor did he attempt to draw a weapon.

"Get down!" commanded Frank. "We've got you covered. Surrender."

Still the rider remained silent.

Frank having quieted the horse went alongside and put his hand on the man's arm.

"Come—" he began, then stopped suddenly.

There was a moment of utter silence, and Frank for the first time in his life could feel the hair rising on his head. Then he controlled himself.

"Put up your rifles boys," he commanded. "The man is dead!"

CHAPTER XI

WITH THE TANKS

"Dead!" exclaimed Frank's comrades in voices that shook with surprise and horror.

"That's what I said," replied Frank. "Touch him and see for yourselves."

All did so and found that the body was rigid. How long the horse had borne his lifeless burden they could not tell. The legs were set stiffly in the stirrups and the hands had a death grip on the reins.

The boys had seen death in many forms. Scarcely a day had passed since their arrival at the front without that sad experience. But it had never seemed so ghastly or uncanny as at this moment. That silent, colossal figure, seated bolt upright, worked fearfully on their imaginations and seemed far more formidable than any living enemy would have seemed.

"One of those bullets that the sentries sent after him must have reached him," said Bart in an awed voice.

"I suppose so," replied Frank. "But it doesn't matter now.

Our search is over."

"What are we going to do with the body?" asked Billy soberly.

"I guess we can't do anything just now," replied Frank. "I don't think we could get those reins out of his hands anyway, and I for one don't want to try. Besides, this is the proof for the officers that the prisoner hasn't escaped. They're anxious, because they don't know what information he might have been carrying back to the German lines. The only thing to do is for one of us to lead the horse—with its rider—back to camp."

This seemed to the others the solution of the problem, although the task was a gruesome one and they would have gladly evaded it if they could. It made chills run down the spine to trudge along leading the horse with that huge figure towering behind them in the darkness, mocking at them because he had escaped to the silent land from which they could never bring him back.

But there was comfort in numbers, and what no one of them could perhaps have done singly they finally accomplished by taking turns, keeping close together all the while as the ghostly cavalcade wound its way through the woods.

It was with a sigh of heartfelt relief that they finally drew up before the friendly lights of the regimental headquarters that had never before seemed so welcome.

Their coming caused a great sensation, and there was soon a dense crowd around them, for the uncanny circumstances of their return spread through the camp like wildfire. The reins were cut from the dead hands and the body lifted to the ground. Then after making a full report the boys went to their quarters. They were besieged with inquiries by curious comrades, but they shook them off as soon as possible. Their experience had been one that they were only too anxious to forget.

"I don't think I want any supper, after all," remarked Tom to his friends.

"Same here," responded Bart. "I don't feel as though I'd ever be hungry again."

"All I want to do is to get to sleep and forget it," said Billy. "That is, if I *can* get to sleep."

"You'll sleep all right," observed Frank, "but I wouldn't guarantee you against nightmare."

But harrowed as their nerves had been, they were too young and healthy to stand out against the sleep they needed, and when they woke the next morning both their spirits and their appetites were as good as usual. Life at the front was too full of work and rush for any one experience to leave its imprint long.

Their first inquiry after breakfast was for Rabig.

"How's Rabig getting along?" Frank asked of Fred Anderson.

"Oh, he's all right, I guess," answered Fred carelessly. "When the doctors came to examine him they found that the wound didn't amount to much. Said he'd be all right in a day or two."

"Is he under arrest?" asked Tom.

"Why, yes, I suppose he is," answered Fred. "But I guess it's a mere form. The fact that the prisoner didn't finally get away will count in his favor. It's like baseball. An error is an error, but if the man who ought to be out at first gets put out when he tries to steal second the error is harmless. It's no credit to Rabig that a bullet got the man he let escape, but it's lucky for him just the same."

It was evident that Anderson had no suspicion that Rabig had been guilty of anything but carelessness, and the boys carefully refrained from saying anything about what they had gathered from their observation the day before. But when they were alone together they had no hesitation about speaking their minds.

"Some fellows could commit murder and get away with it," grumbled Tom.

"Cheer up, you old grouch," chaffed Billy. "At any rate the prisoner didn't escape, and so there's no harm done."

"And if Rabig is guilty he's got nothing from it but a sore head," put in Bart.

"I don't feel dead sure that Rabig helped him," said Frank, "and yet the more I think it over, the more I'm inclined to think that Tom is right about it. Still, Rabig's entitled to the benefit of the doubt. I know how the Scotch jury felt when they brought in the verdict: 'Not guilty, but don't do it again.'"

"That's just what I'm afraid Rabig will do," said Tom. "This time luckily it didn't matter. The prisoner didn't escape. But if Rabig is a traitor, how do we know but what the next time he might do something that might cause a defeat?"

"It does make one uneasy," agreed Bart. "Nick in the

regiment is like a splinter in the finger. It makes you sore. But we'll keep our eyes open and the very next crooked move he makes it will be curtains for him."

"Or taps," added Billy.

The fighting now had lost the first intensity that had signalized the day of the mine explosion. The Germans had been strongly reinforced, and had held their third line, which had now become their first.

"And they've got plenty of other lines behind that one," commented Tom, as he sat on a trench step cleaning and oiling his rifle.

"Slathers of them," assented Billy. "I suppose they stretch all the way back to the Rhine."

"It will be some job to root them out of them if we have to storm each one of them in turn," remarked Bart.

"We don't have to count on that," said Frank confidently. "The Allies gained twenty-five miles at a clip when they drove Hindenburg back from the Somme. The Huns may stand out a long while, but when the time comes they may collapse all at once like the deacon's 'one-hoss shay.'"

The Americans in the meantime had thoroughly reorganized the captured positions and had held them against a number of strong counter-attacks. But these became fewer as they failed to produce results, and although the artillery still kept on growling and barking, the wearied infantry had a chance to get some of the rest they so sorely needed after their herculean efforts.

"Nothing to do till to-morrow," yawned Billy, as after

performing their turn of trench duty they found themselves with an hour or two on their hands.

"Let's take a little hike back of the lines and see what's doing," suggested Bart.

"I think there's something in the wind connected with the tanks," remarked Frank. "They say there's a bunch of them coming up from all parts of the front and getting together just back of our division."

"They're hot playthings, all right," commented Tom. "They certainly keep the Huns on the jump. If we only had enough of them we might roll right into Berlin."

They passed some of the field batteries where the men, stripped to the waist, were serving the guns, running the shells in and discharging their weapons with marvelous smoothness, speed and precision.

"This is the life," chaffed Tom. "You fellows have a picnic here away back of the lines, while we chaps in the front line do all the work and stop all the bullets."

"G'wan, you doughboys," retorted a gunner good-naturedly. "If we're alive here after eight days, the orders are to shoot us for loafing."

A little further on, they came upon a myriad of tanks of all descriptions. There were "baby" tanks, "whippets," "male" and "female," all with different functions to perform during a battle. Just as in the navy there are vessels of all sizes from a light scout to a super-dreadnought, so already this arm of the service was developing various grades, each to do some special work for which the others were not so well adapted.

"See how they're hidden," said Frank, as he pointed to a very forest of bushes and branches that extended above the array of tanks.

"That's to keep the Boche aviators guessing," observed Bart. "They'd give their eyes if they could only spy out where these fellows are being massed."

"I heard one of the fellows say that the tanks travel only at night so that the Boches can't track them," said Tom.

"And see what a raft of them have been got together here," said Billy. "I tell you, fellows, there's something big going to be pulled off before long."

"Say, boys, see who's here!" exclaimed Frank, and they turned to see Will Stone coming toward them with a broad smile of welcome on his bronzed face.

CHAPTER XII

BREAKING THROUGH

There was a rush toward Will Stone, and in a moment the Army boys were shaking hands with a vigor that showed the pleasure they felt at again meeting their acquaintance, who belonged to the tank division.

"Say, fellows, have a heart," Will grinned. "I need these hands in my business. But it sure does me good to see you again. And all of you alive and kicking! I'll bet that's more than some of the Huns are that you've run up against."

"Oh, we're still able to sit up and take nourishment," laughed Frank. "But tell us about yourself, old man. You look like ready money."

"I see you have a marking different from what you had when we saw you last," remarked Bart, looking at the insignia that proclaimed Will an officer.

"And look at that war cross!" cried Tom. "I guess you've been some busy little bee to get that. Shake again, old scout."

Stone flushed and looked a little embarrassed.

"Only a few little skirmishes here and there," he said deprecatingly. "But the real big thing is yet to come. Look at this army of tanks. We've never had so many in one place since the war began."

"Looks like a herd of elephants," commented Frank, as his eye ran along the array that seemed to number hundreds. "They'll do more trampling than any herd of elephants that ever trod the earth," remarked Stone grimly. "But come along, fellows, and let me show you my own particular pet. It's the biggest one of the bunch, and it's a peach! We call it Jumbo, and it carries a crew of twenty men."

They followed him till they came to a monster tank on which Stone placed his hand caressingly.

"Isn't it a beauty?" he asked, as he beamed upon them.

"I should call it a holy terror," grinned Frank.

"What the Huns will call it won't be fit for publication," laughed Billy.

"I guess they've already exhausted the German vocabulary," chuckled Stone. "But just wait until this beauty of mine goes climbing over their trenches and smashing their pill boxes and tearing away their entanglements. Then they'll know what they're up against."

"I only wish we could see you while you're doing it," remarked Tom.

"Likely enough you will," replied Stone. "From things I've picked up here and there I think the infantry will be right alongside of us in the next big jamboree. Don't you fellows make any mistake about it, there's going to be one of the biggest stunts of the war pulled off in the course of the next few days. Mithridates with his elephants won't be a circumstance to us with our tanks. There sure is bound to be some lovely fighting."

"Let it come!" exclaimed Tom.

"And come quickly," chimed in Frank.

"The only thing I'm sorry for is that you're in the Canadian contingent," said Bart. "I want to see you leading the way in a U. S. A. tank."

"You may yet," replied Stone. "Uncle Sam will soon be sending over his tanks, and you bet when they do come they'll be lallapaloozers with all the modern improvements, and then some! And the minute that happens I'm going to apply to be transferred to the United States army. These Canadians are among the finest men in the world and they're doing magnificent fighting, but still I'll feel more natural when I'm fighting under the Stars and Stripes."

"Well, that won't be long now," replied Frank. "Our men and our guns and our tanks and everything else we need to lick the Kaiser will be coming in droves pretty soon. And then watch our smoke."

"Right you are," agreed Stone enthusiastically.

Then as a trumpet rang out he added: "That's the signal for a rehearsal, fellows, and I'll have to get on the job. We're going to put our machines through their paces. I'm mighty glad to have seen you again, and I wish you no end of luck."

"Come over to our line when you get a chance and see the way our boys are shaping up," was Frank's invitation, which was echoed heartily by the others.

"You bet I will," responded Stone, as with a wave of his hand he went to his work, while the boys strolled back to their quarters.

"He's the real stuff," commented Frank. "All wool and a yard wide."

"He'd rather fight than eat," observed Tom.

"If the Canadians take him as a sample, no wonder they're glad to see Uncle Sam mix in," remarked Billy.

Some days went by, days of steady rush and preparation. It was evident that some big operation was near at hand. Troops were moved up from other portions of the long line that stretched from Switzerland to the sea. There were the bronzed Tommies in khaki, the snappy, dashing poilus in their uniforms of corn-flower blue, veterans hardened in a score of battles from Ypres to Verdun. And right alongside of them in closest comradeship and gallant rivalry were the stalwart sons of the United States of America, the very flower of her youth, who had already had their baptism of fire and who had sworn to themselves that no flag should be further in the van than Old Glory when it came to the stern test of battle.

Nearer and nearer the tanks had crept to the front of the line and taken up their places in front of great openings that had been made in the wire entanglements and skilfully concealed from the enemy.

A certain number of them were assigned to lead each regiment, and the Camport boys' delight was great when they saw that Jumbo, with a squad of assisting tanks, had been told off to lead their regiment.

"Just what the doctor ordered," exulted Frank, when he saw Stone step out of the door of the monster tank.

"We'll follow you, old man, till the cows come home," called Bart, as the boys crowded around the young operator.

"We'll try to make a broad path for you," laughed Stone, as he returned their greeting cordially.

"When is the show coming off?" asked Billy.

"Almost any time now, I guess," replied Stone. "About all we need is a nice misty morning. It's up to the weather sharps to tip us off. Then we'll amble over and give the Huns a little shaking up."

Several days passed with the weather exasperatingly clear. Usually the soldiers would have welcomed the bright sunny mornings. But now, when they were keyed up to a high pitch, the one thing they longed for was a dull and lowering sky that would favor the great enterprise they had on hand.

"You might think the boys were a lot of grangers after a dry spell, from the way they're praying for rain," remarked Billy, as for the hundredth time he scanned the sky.

"Remember how different it used to be when we had a baseball game on hand?" laughed Frank. "Then a gleam of sunshine was like money from home after you'd been broke for a week."

"That cloud a little while ago looked as though it might have had thunder and lightning behind it," observed Bart, "but it was only a false alarm."

"Nothing but wind, like a German bulletin," grinned Billy, stretching himself.

"Or their U-boat prophecies," added Frank. "But cheer up, fellows, this sunshine can't last forever."

There came at last just the kind of weather wanted. A soft drizzle set in at nightfall, not enough to make the ground muddy, but enough to make the steaming and saturated air lie heavy on the earth. Everything indicated that there would be a fog at dawn.

"I guess to-morrow's the big day," remarked Frank, as he looked out at the settling mists.

"High time," grumbled Tom. "I'd grow stale if we had to wait much longer."

The regiments slept on their arms that night, and an hour before dawn all were astir and in their places. There was no special artillery fire, such as usually preceded big attacks. It was given to the tanks to level the entanglements of the enemy and open up the gaps for the troops to swarm through.

The hour dragged by until within ten minutes of the time appointed for the assault. Then a monotonous hum filled the air as the motors of the tanks tuned up. Down through the black lines of waiting soldiers the gray monsters slowly made their way, passed through the gaps made in the defences and led the way into the desolate stretch of No Man's Land.

Even to the friendly eyes that watched them there was something weird and frightful in their aspect. It was as though the huge brutes of the prehistoric world had taken form before them. Even those monsters had never carried within them such death-dealing power.

As the sea closes in the wake of a ship, the troops fell in behind the tanks, and the silent procession took up the march toward the German lines.

Hardly a sound beyond the labored breathing of the tanks broke the stillness. It might have been an army of ghosts.

On they went, and with every step the conviction grew that the surprise would be complete. No thunder broke from the enemy guns. No fiery barrage swept the dense ranks, exacting its toll of wounds and death. For once the Hun was asleep.

Nearer and nearer. Then like so many thunderbolts at a hundred different points they struck the German lines and the tanks went through!

CHAPTER XIII

CAUGHT NAPPING

Nothing could stand before the terrific impact of the war tanks.

There was a grinding, tearing, screeching sound, as wire entanglements were uprooted. These had been strengthened in every way that German cunning could invent, but they bent like straws beneath the onslaught of the gray monsters. A cyclone could not have done the work more thoroughly.

There was no need now for further secrecy, and with a wild yell the Allied troops swarmed through the gaps, sending a deadly volley before them, supplemented by thousands of grenades.

At the same instant, the Allied artillery opened up and laid a heavy barrage fire over the heads of the onrushing troops.

The blow came down on the Germans with crushing force. The surprise was complete. Every detail of the great drive had been mapped out with the precision of clockwork, and so nicely had it been timed that on every part of the long line the shock came like a thunderbolt.

A horde of Germans rushed up from the trenches and poured in a great stream into the open. The earth seemed to disgorge itself. They came shouting and yelling in wild consternation, their eyes heavy with sleep and their faces pallid with fear.

Fear not so much of the Allied troops rushing upon them. These they had faced in many battles, and though they knew the mettle of their foes, they were still men who could be faced on even terms. But their courage gave way when through the spectral mists they saw the wallowing monsters bearing down on them like so many Juggernauts, crushing, tearing, mowing them down as though they were insects in the path of giants.

The men fled helter-skelter in the wildest panic that had come upon them since the outbreak of the war. In vain their officers shouted and cursed at them. The iron bonds of discipline snapped like threads. Soldiers rushed hither and thither like ants whose hill had been demolished by a ruthless foot.

Many fled back toward their second line, pursued by a withering blast of rifle fire that reaped a terrible harvest of wounds and death. Others rushed back into their trenches, crowding and treading upon one another. But even here they were not safe from the great tanks, which lumbered down into the trenches and up on the other side, leaving devastation in their wake, spitting out flame from the guns they carried, while they themselves in their iron armor went on uninjured.

Not only were they frightful engines of offense, but they served as well for defense of the troops that followed after them.

For the first few minutes the slaughter was awful, and it

looked as though the whole German line would be forced to give way without putting up any resistance worthy of the name. Prisoners were rounded up by the hundreds. There was no time then to send them to the rear. So they were gathered together in the open spaces, their suspenders were cut so that their trousers would slip down and entangle their legs if they tried to escape in the confusion, a small guard was put over them, and the tanks and the troops went thundering on toward the second line.

But here the resistance began to stiffen. The first paralysis of surprise was past. The heavy guns of the enemy opened up, and from scores of machine gun nests and pill boxes came a storm of bullets. The German officers had got their troops under some semblance of control, and heavy reinforcements were rushed up from the rear. From now on the Allies had an awakened and powerful foe to reckon with.

But despite the sterner opposition, the tanks were not to be denied. On they went, as resistless as fate. Their sides were reddened now, and the wake they left behind them was fearful to look upon.

Through the second line entanglements they crashed as easily as through the first, although this time they met with losses. Some had overturned and others had been struck by heavy shells and put out of action. But even though disabled, the guns on one side or the other were still able to pour out their messengers of death and take savage toll of the enemy.

Jumbo was leading, and close behind followed the boys of the old Thirty-seventh, with Frank and his chums in the van. They were fighting like young Vikings, their rifles empty but their bayonets and hand grenades doing deadly work. Their arms were tired by their terrific efforts, but their hearts were on fire. They felt as though they were treading on air, and the blood ran through their veins like quicksilver. Bunker Hill and Gettysburg spoke through them. The traditions of a hundred glorious battlefields on which Americans had fought was theirs. Now again Americans were fighting, fighting to avenge the murdered women and babies of the Lusitania, fighting to crush the most barbarous tyranny the modern world has known, fighting the battle of freedom and civilization.

So they fought on like demons, smashing a pill box here, routing out a machine gun nest there, until the second line was carried. Then the conquerors paused for breath.

On the whole German front in that region two lines deep the line had been smashed. That crowded hour of stark fighting had cracked the boasted invincible line of Hindenburg and sent the foe flying in confusion toward their third and most formidable line. Thousands of prisoners and scores of guns were among the spoils of victory.

And the most gratifying feature of the drive was the insignificant loss to the Allied forces. The resistance at first had been only slight, and even in the second phase of the battle it had been so quickly overcome that few of the attacking troops had fallen. Seldom had so great an advance been made at so small a price.

But modern warfare has its limits in the matter of time and speed. The very swiftness with which they had advanced had in itself an element of danger because it had brought them too far ahead of their supporting guns. These had to be brought up from the rear, and the captured positions had to be reorganized. The troops, too, had to be given a breathing spell, for they had reached the limit of human endurance.

So a halt was called, and the wearied men took turns in

resting and refreshing themselves for the hard work that still lay ahead of them.

"A mighty good morning's work," panted Frank, as he threw himself down at the roots of a giant tree which had been utterly stripped of branches and even of bark by the tempest of fire that had raged around it.

"Ask a German and see if he'd agree with you," said Billy with a grin.

"We've got plenty to ask," said Tom, as his eyes roved over the throng of prisoners. "We sure have taken a raft of them this morning. And there's a still bigger bunch that will never answer roll call again."

There was food in plenty, but they did not have to avail themselves of the rations they carried in their kits. There were the camp kitchens of the enemy that in a twinkling were set to work, and soon the savory odors of steaming stews and fragrant coffee filled the smoke-laden air and brought joy to the hearts of the victors.

Frank, Bart, Billy and Tom were lucky enough to stumble on a meal that had already been started for some German officers, and they were surprised to find it so good and abundant.

"The Germans may be starving, but there's no sign of it here," remarked Frank, as he threw himself down on the ground with a sigh of relief.

"Trust the Huns to look after their soldiers, even if the civilians starve," replied Bart. "The people don't count in Germany. Only the military are taken seriously. They take the middle of the sidewalk and others are crowded to the wall."

"Well, I'm not quarreling with them just now on that account," grinned Billy. "I'm just glad there's plenty of grub here this morning."

"I'm not very partial to German cooking as a rule," chuckled Tom, "but this stew certainly smells good. How the Boche officers would grit their teeth if they saw us wading into this."

But his rejoicing was premature, for just at this moment a cannon shot from the German lines tore its way through the kettle and the scalding broth was spattered all over the group that were lying about. Luckily it did no other damage, but the chagrin of the boys was comical to see.

"I'd like to have hold of the gunner that fired that shot," sputtered Tom wrathfully, as he wiped from his face some of the stew that had fallen to his share.

"You ought to have knocked wood when you talked of the German officers seeing us wading into their chow," growled Bart. "There's a perfectly good stew gone to the dogs."

"Nothing personal in that, I hope," laughed Frank, "because most of it came to us."

"I like mine inside," put in Billy, as he gingerly removed a piece of meat from his ear. "As an outside decoration I'm dead against stew."

"Well, cheer up, fellows," remarked Frank. "The stew's past praying for, but there's a lot of other things. And anyway we ought to be mighty thankful that the shot didn't remove some of us from the landscape as well as the kettle."

"What's the big noise about?" asked a cheery voice, and they looked up to see Will Stone regarding them with a quizzical grin.

CHAPTER XIV

IN CLOSE QUARTERS

The four Camport boys greeted Stone joyfully and gladly made room for him.

"It's another German atrocity," grinned Billy. "They were sore at us for swiping their grub and they sent our kettle to smithereens."

"I'm glad they don't know about it anyway," said Tom. "I don't want any Boche to have the laugh on me."

"I guess they're not doing much laughing this morning," remarked Will Stone, as he dropped down on the ground beside them. "Or if they are, it's on the wrong side of their mouths."

"We've certainly waxed them good and plenty," said Bart enthusiastically.

"Jumbo was all to the good this morning," exulted Frank. "It did my heart good to see the way he ploughed along. There was nothing to it after he got started."

"He certainly scattered the Huns good and plenty," chortled

Billy. "They ran like hares."

"He does for 'em all right," agreed Stone, glad to have his pride in his giant pet justified. "And the best of it is that, although the bullets came against his hide like hail on a tin roof, he came through practically without a scratch. He sure is a tough old fellow."

"The tanks are wonders," chimed in Tom. "They've won this fight. It was scrumptious the way they tore those entanglements up by the roots. Without 'em we'd have lost ten times as many men as we did."

"So far we've gotten off pretty easily," agreed Stone, "but the hardest part of the fighting is coming. The Boches have got their second wind by this time, and there can't be any more surprises. You fellows would better fill up now, for you'll have to have plenty to stand up on."

"Trust us," laughed Billy. "We may be slow in some things, but when it comes to filling up, we're some pumpkins. But I certainly do feel sore about that stew."

"Billy'll never get over that," laughed Bart. "He had his mouth all fixed for it. No other stew in all his life will ever taste so good to him as this one that he didn't get."

"It's always the biggest fish that gets away," laughed Stone, as he fell to with the rest.

While they were eating, there was a thunder of hoofs along the road. This had been such an unusual occurrence up to date that they sprang to their feet with eager interest.

Then the cavalry swept by.

Fine fellows the cavalrymen were on splendid mounts, which they bestrode as though they had never done anything else in all their lives. For months past they had chafed under restraint, for since the struggle had settled down to trench warfare they had seldom seen service except on foot. But now their turn had come, for with the broken line of the enemy had come a call for the cavalry to pursue and complete the demoralization of the foe.

"Some class to that bunch," remarked Tom, as he watched the flying column with an appraising eye.

"A little faster than your tanks, old scout?" remarked Bart, giving Stone a nudge in the ribs.

"They sure are," admitted Stone. "But don't forget that though we may be slow we get there just the same."

After a brief resting spell the lines were reformed and the fighting was resumed. The space between the second and the third lines was a wide one, and the country was hilly, with numerous lanes and ravines. These were being held in greater or less force by enemy troops posted in advantageous positions supported by machine guns, while beyond them their big guns kept up a heavy fire to prevent the Allied advance.

To clean these up and get ready for an attack upon the third line was a work of hours, as every foot of advance was bitterly contested by the Germans, who had now recovered from their surprise and fought desperately to stem the tide that had overwhelmed their first position.

There were two or three villages in the fighting zone and one town of considerable size. Not that it was a town now in any real sense of the word. What had once been houses were now mere pitiful heaps of wood and stone and mortar, and their inhabitants had long since been dispossessed or slain. It stood gaunt and desolate and forbidding in its mute protest against the pitiless storm of war to which it had fallen a victim.

In cleaning out a particularly obnoxious nest of machine gun positions Frank and his friends had been kept busy until nearly noon. But at last the guns were silenced and the crews wiped out or captured.

The boys started to regain their main force, but the country was unfamiliar and they took a turning in the road which led toward the German lines instead of toward their own.

"Gee!" remarked Tom as they trudged along, "maybe I'm not tired. My feet feel as though they weighed a ton."

"Perhaps they do," gibed Billy unfeelingly. "Considering the size of them, I should say a ton was just about right."

"I notice your hoofs are not so small," retorted Tom. "But how much longer is this hike going to take?"

"Search me," responded Frank. "To tell the truth, I'm twisted up about the direction. Seems to me we ought to strike some of our troops soon."

"It would be funny if we walked straight into the German lines," observed Billy.

"Funny!" snorted Tom. "Yes, as funny as a funeral. Some people have a queer sense of humor."

They were passing a hedge that walled off an orchard from the road when Frank, who was ahead, saw before him a great wave of gray uniforms coming around a bend in the road.

"Quick, fellows," he whispered. "Over the hedge and down on the ground."

Like a flash the boys were out of sight, and not one instant too soon, for a moment later they could see through the hedge what seemed to be an endless line of gray uniforms going past at the double quick. They were evidently hurrying forward to reinforce their hard-pressed comrades farther down the road.

The boys lay still as death until the troops had passed, and then looked at each other ruefully.

"We're cut off," ejaculated Frank. "Those fellows are between us and our line."

"Looks pretty bad," said Bart.

"This is a pretty kettle of fish," grumbled Tom. "Let's cut across the orchard and see if we can find some of our boys."

They acted on the suggestion, but found to their dismay that the Germans were everywhere. In whatever direction they looked the only uniforms they saw were the detested field gray. The Germans had rallied and the boys had been caught in the swirl of the returning tide.

"We'll have to hide somewhere until our men drive back the Huns and get as far as this orchard," said Billy.

"We're up against it for fair," growled Tom disconsolately.

"It's easy enough to talk of hiding, but where shall we hide?" asked Bart. "If we stay here above ground we're bound to be spotted before long."

"Let's make our way toward the town," suggested Frank. "There wasn't a soul in sight there a few minutes ago. It seemed to be wholly deserted. There must be plenty of hiding places in those heaps of stones, or perhaps we can stow ourselves away in a cellar. Let's get a hustle on, too, or we'll know sooner than we want to what a prison camp looks like."

As quickly as they dared they crept along, using every bit of cover that offered itself until they reached the outskirts of what had been the town. As Frank had said, it appeared to be wholly deserted at the moment. It was clear that all available forces had been summoned away to stem the great drive.

Having satisfied themselves that there was no one about they moved cautiously from one street to another seeking some place of refuge. The prospect was not hopeful, for there was scarcely a room in a single house that was not gaping wide open. Doors were gone and windows had vanished. There was hardly a place where anything as large as a cat could be free from detection.

"A mighty slim outlook," grumbled Tom, as they crouched close to a pile of masonry near the corner of a street.

"Stop grouching," counseled Frank. "We may stumble across something at any minute."

"Stumble is right," said Bart, as he rubbed a barked shin. "I've been doing nothing else since we got in among these rock piles."

"That house over the way there seems in a little better condition than the rest of these heaps," suggested Billy, pointing a little way down the street.

"We'll try our luck there," said Frank, and again their cautious journey was resumed.

They reached the place and squeezed themselves in through a narrow opening on a side that had faced a tiny yard bordered by a wall about eight feet in height.

There had been three rooms on the ground floor of the house, but all three had been knocked into one by the visitation of shells. The boys picked their way over the uneven masses of plaster, and Frank gave an exclamation as he perceived an opening that seemed to lead down into a cellar.

"This way, fellows," he said as he looked down into the darkness. "I don't see any stairs here but we can take a chance and drop. It doesn't seem very deep. One of you hold this gun of mine and I'll go first."

There was a chance of spraining an ankle if nothing worse, but luckily he landed safely.

"All serene," he called up in a low tone. "Hand me down your guns and then come along."

They did so, and the four found themselves in a cluttered cellar that by feeling around with their hands they found to be about thirty feet long by twenty in width. There was a furnace which had been broken into a pile of junk and a little light filtering down showed where a pipe had formerly gone through to the upper floor. There were a number of barrels in one corner, but apart from these the cellar seemed to hold nothing but rubbish.

"It's as dark as Egypt down here," grumbled Tom.

"So much the better," replied Bart. "There'll be that much less chance of a Heinie seeing us if he takes the trouble to look down here."

"So this is where we've got to hang out until our boys get here," remarked Billy, grinning. "It reminds me of the Waldorf-Astoria—it's so different."

"Never mind," said Frank cheerfully, "it's a thousand per cent. better than a Hun prison camp, and don't you forget it!"

"You said a mouthful that time," replied the irrepressible Billy, with more force than elegance.

CHAPTER XV

THE FOUR-FOOTED ENEMY

"The first thing to do is to make a barricade of these barrels," said Frank, when the four privates had made an inventory of what the cellar afforded in the way of defense.

"They will help us in putting up a fight if the Huns discover us here," agreed Bart.

"Let's see if there's anything in them," suggested Billy.

"Swell chance," commented Tom. "They smell as if they'd had wine or beer in them, and you can trust the Heinies to have drained them to the last drop. Not that I want any of the stuff, but if they were full they'd stop a bullet better than if they were empty."

They tested the barrels by knocking against them with the butts of their rifles and the hollow sound they gave back proved that Tom had conjectured truly.

"Dry as the Desert of Sahara," pronounced Frank.

"And that reminds me," said Bart. "What are we going to do for water to drink? We've got grub enough in our kits to last us a couple of days in a pinch. But we can't hold out long without something to wash it down with."

"We won't worry about that yet," said Frank. "I stepped into a puddle over in one corner while we were going round here. I suppose that came from the rain we had last night. It doesn't fit my idea of what drinking water ought to be, but it's a mighty sight better than dying of thirst."

They got out their stock of food and decided that with careful rationing they had enough for two days.

"And that will be plenty," prophesied Billy. "Our fellows will be here before long. Perhaps this very night we'll be with the old bunch again."

"I wish I had your cheery disposition," growled Tom. "When any one hands you a lemon—"

"I make lemonade out of it," came back Billy, and there was a general laugh.

"That's the way to talk," said Frank. "The Huns haven't got us yet, and even this hole is better than a German prison camp."

"You bet!" responded Billy. "From all I hear those places are something fierce. A fellow had better die fighting than die of abuse or starvation."

"That's what," agreed Bart. "And that's another thing that shows how low the Huns have stooped in this war. Look at the way we treat them when we take them prisoners. They live on the fat of the land. Of course the Germans haven't as much food in their country as we have, and we don't expect so much for our men in the matter of grub, although even at that they don't get enough to keep body and soul together. But it's sickening to hear of the way they torture them. One of their favorite sports is to set dogs on 'em. If a man doesn't move quickly enough to suit 'em they stick a bayonet into him. It's low beastly tyranny that puts them on a level with the Turks. It's no wonder that Germany is coming to be hated and despised by the whole world."

"Did you hear of the fire that happened in one of their camps?" queried Tom. "There was a hut in one corner of the camp with five men in it. It caught fire and the men, who couldn't get out of the door because it was locked, tried to get out of the window. The sentry thrust his bayonet into the first man, and threw him back into the flames. The poor fellow made another attempt and again the sentry ran the bayonet into him. And every one of the five men burned to death, though every one of them could have been saved. What do you think of that, fellows? Isn't it the limit?"

"They'll get theirs," said Frank bitterly. "They can't sow the wind without reaping the whirlwind. They'll surely pay, soon or late, for every bit of this brutality.

"I hope it will be soon," said Billy. "I'm getting impatient."

"It won't be long if we can keep up the pace we set this morning," said Bart. "Gee, how our tanks went through those wires as though they were rotten cord."

"And our guns are keeping it up," said Frank. "Just listen to that roar. What a shame it is we can't be out there doing our bit. It makes me feel like a slacker."

"It's the fortune of war," said Billy philosophically. "But it's might hard luck just the same that we took the wrong direction after we cleared up that machine gun nest so neatly.

But let's have a hack at that grub, fellows. Oh, boy, if we only had some of that stew we lost this morning!"

"That stew still sticks in Billy's crop," laughed Frank.

"I only wish it did," mourned Billy. "But it never got that far."

"Well, just remember, fellows, that we're on rations now," warned Frank as he doled out a little portion to each from the common stock they had pooled together. "We've got to make this last as long as we can. If we feel hungry when we get through we'll just have to tighten our belts and let it go at that."

They ate sparingly, but, although they were all thirsty, especially after the heat and excitement of the fighting, it was a long time before they could bring themselves to drink from the pool in the corner of the cellar. They finally had to come to it, however, though they tried to make it less repugnant by filtering it through the only clean handkerchief they could muster among them.

The time dragged on interminably in their narrow quarters. They tried to sleep, but though they were very tired after their strenuous day, the novelty and discomfort of their position kept them on edge.

The daylight finally vanished from the little opening in the floor above and the darkness became absolute. They had matches in their kits, but they feared to use them lest some prowling sentry might see the light through some rift in the masonry.

The roar of the heavy artillery had died down, though the guns still gave out an occasional challenge. The fighting for the day was evidently at an end. But there had been no clash in the streets of the ruined town to betoken the arrival of the Allied forces. However they might have fared in other parts of the battlefield, the town itself had not been wrested from the Germans. In all probability the boys were still in the midst of their enemies.

"Another night as well as a day to stay in this shebang," remarked Tom when the hope of immediate rescue had failed them.

"Oh, well, to-morrow's a new day," said Frank. "A lot may happen between now and to-morrow night. Our grub will hold out till then anyway, and if nothing better turns up we'll make a dash and try to reach our lines."

He had scarcely stopped speaking when there was a loud clattering in the street as though a cavalry troop were passing through.

"Perhaps those are our men now!" exclaimed Billy jubilantly.

"Perhaps," assented Frank. "And they seem to be coming this way."

The pace of the horses died down as they neared the house, and they finally stopped just before it. The boys could hear the troopers dismount and a moment later they heard footsteps on the floor above.

They listened intently. Would the first words they heard be English or German? If the first it would mean a boisterous shout to the men above and a hasty and joyful scramble out of their prison. If the second, it would mean that they were in imminent danger of capture or death.

A light filtered down through the hole where the stovepipe had been. Somebody above had struck a match. But he had evidently burned his fingers as he did so, for the light went out and there was an impatient exclamation.

"*Donnerwetter*!"

Just one word, but it made the hearts of the listening boys go down into their boots.

For it was a German who just then struck a second match and lighted a candle, and it was a German cavalry troop whose horses stood before the door.

But for what purpose had they entered the house? Were they in search of the boys? Had any one seen them entering the house and given information?

"Be ready, fellows," whispered Frank. "It looks as if we were in for a scrap."

They clutched their rifles firmly to be ready for whatever might happen.

But it was not long before they realized that this sudden irruption had nothing to do with them. What seemed to be a bench or a table was dragged across the floor and one or more candles placed upon it. There seemed to be half a dozen or more officers in the room, and they were soon engaged in an earnest conversation.

"I never thought much of the German language," whispered Bart to Billy, "but I'd give a farm to understand it now."

"If Frank only knew German as well as he does French," responded Billy, "we might pick up something that our officers would give a lot to know."

For perhaps half an hour the raucous tones above continued. The debate was at times an angry one and was punctuated by the sound of fists brought heavily down on a table. Just after one of these, the stovepipe hole was dimmed by something that shut off the light from the room above. It floated down with a slight rustle and the boys could see that it was a paper of some kind.

In an instant Frank had crept across and grabbed the paper, thrusting it into the bosom of his shirt. Then he moved swiftly back to the shelter of the barricade.

"That was taking a chance, old boy," whispered Bart, as his friend resumed his place among them. "If you'd knocked against anything and the Huns had heard you, they'd have been down here in a jiffy."

"I suppose it was a little risky," returned Frank, "but we've got to take risks sometimes, and it struck me that there might be something in that paper that our officers would like to know."

Just then Billy, in trying to get in a less cramped position, knocked against one of the rifles that had been stood in a corner. It fell against one of the barrels with a clatter that in the confined place and the tense state of the boys' nerves sounded to them like thunder.

Frank grabbed it before it could fall on the cellar floor, but it seemed as though the mischief must have been done, and their hearts were in their mouths as they listened for anything that might indicate that the sound had been heard on the floor above.

But the debate had reached a lively stage just at that moment, and the incident attracted no attention, so that after two minutes more of strained listening the boys were assured that they had come off scot free from what might have been a disaster.

"This is sure no place for a man with heart disease," murmured Tom, and his comrades unanimously agreed with him.

The conference in the room above had come to an end, as was shown by the shuffling of feet as the men rose from the table. There was a sound as of a sheaf of papers being hastily gathered together. But there was no outcry to indicate that any one of them was missing, and the boys drew a long breath and relaxed their grasp on their rifles. There would be no search, and for the moment they were safe.

The lights above were extinguished and the party went out. The horses clattered away, and once more the house and the town were as still as the grave.

"So near and yet so far," murmured Frank, when he was sure that the last of the unwelcome visitors had departed.

"That was what you might call too close for comfort," grinned Billy.

"They wouldn't have done a thing to us if they had nabbed us," declared Bart. "We wouldn't have had a Chinaman's chance. No prison camp for ours! They'd have shot us down like dogs! They'd have reasoned that we had heard their military plans, and that would have been all the excuse they wanted."

"Not that they would care whether they had the excuse or

not," said Billy. "The mere fact that a German wants to do anything makes it all right to do it."

"How they'd froth at the mouth if they knew Frank had that paper," remarked Tom. "I wonder what it is."

"It has a seal on it and it feels as if it were heavy and official," replied Frank. "I don't want to strike a match now, but I'll take a squint at it when daylight comes. Probably it's in German, and if it is I can't read it. But they'll read it at headquarters all right, and it may queer some of Heinie's plans."

They conversed in whispers a little while longer, and then made ready to go to sleep. Their preparations were not extensive, and consisted chiefly in finding a place where no sharp edge of stone bored into the small of their backs. But they were too tired to be critical, and after putting away the food in a corner and arranging to stand watch turn and turn about they soon forgot their troubles in sleep.

When they awoke the light shining through the hole in the floor told them that it was day.

"Time you fellows opened your eyes," remarked Tom, who had been standing the last watch. "If you hadn't I'd have booted you awake anyway, for you were snoring loud enough to bring the whole German army down on you."

"I'd hate to call you an out and out prevaricator, Tom," remarked Billy, rubbing his eyes and running his hands through his tumbled hair, "so I'll simply say that you use the truth with great economy. Suppose you bring me my breakfast. I think I'll eat it in bed this morning."

He dodged the shoe that Tom threw at his head and rose

laughingly to his feet.

"Mighty bad manners the people have at this hotel," he remarked, "but since you feel that way about it I'll take my grub any way I can get it. Haul it out from that corner, Bart, and let's have a hack at it. I'm hungry enough to eat nails this morning."

Bart needed no second request, for he was quite as hungry as his mates. But when he picked up the canvas wrapper in which the food had been stored he dropped it with a startled exclamation.

"What's the matter?" cried Frank.

"Matter enough," replied Bart. "The bag's empty. There isn't a blessed thing in it."

The others rushed him under the light that came from above and examined the wrapper with sinking hearts. What Bart had said was true. Not a crumb was left.

There was no mystery about it. The gnawed and tattered holes in the bag told their own story. It was summed up in the one word that came from their lips simultaneously. "Rats!"

Their four-footed enemies had perhaps brought them nearer capture than their human enemies had been able to do.

CHAPTER XVI

CHASED BY CAVALRY

The four Army boys looked at each other in dismay.

Nothing much worse than this could have befallen them. It brought them close to the edge of tragedy. They would have to change their plans. Instead of being free to choose their own time for their attempt to escape, they were forced to act quickly no matter how much greater the risk might be. For if they waited until they were weak from hunger they would be in no condition to make a dash or put up a fight.

Frank as usual was the first to recover his self-possession.

"No use crying over spilt milk, fellows," he said, trying to infuse cheerfulness into his tone. "We've got to try Billy's recipe and make lemonade from the lemon that the rats have handed us."

"It's a mighty big lemon," said Tom, "and I don't see much sugar lying around."

"How could the brutes have got at it without our hearing them, do you suppose?" questioned Bart.

"That doesn't matter much," replied Billy. "And there's no use holding post-mortems. The thing is, what are we going to do?"

"We're going to get out of here to-night without fail," said Frank decidedly. "The moon won't come up till late and if the night is cloudy it won't show up at all. At any rate we can't stay here. There isn't a chance on earth of there being anything left in these houses, or we might take a chance on foraging. The Huns have seen to that. The longer we stay here the weaker we'll get. We've just got to make a break and trust our wits and our luck to get back to the lines."

"I guess you're right, old man," agreed Bart. "We'll just move our belts up a hole and pretend we're not hungry. Tom here's getting too fat anyway, and it'll do him good to give his stomach a rest. And as for Billy, he can take a nap and dream of that stew he didn't get."

"There's another thing, too," remarked Frank. "Those rats are likely to come back to-night for more, and they may have spread the news and bring a whole rat colony with them. No doubt they're famished since there's nothing left in the town to eat, and if there are enough of them they might go for us. Of course we could beat them off, but we'd be apt to make a lot of noise in doing it, and that might bring the Huns down on us. There's no use talking, we've got to skip."

They all agreed to this, and they passed the rest of that day as best they could until the light faded from the hole in the floor and night settled down in a pall of velvet. They clambered out of their temporary prison, their hearts beating with high determination.

They ventured out at last into the darkness, slipping along from one projection of the ruined houses to another, moving as lightly and stealthily as cats.

To one thing they had made up their minds. There would be no going back to their old hiding place. That meant either starvation or surrender. Besides, if they turned back on being discovered, the Germans would know that they were hiding somewhere in the ruined town and they would not leave one stone on another until they found them. But if they made a break for the open country they would have their chance of escaping in the darkness. On they went like so many spectres, until, on reaching a shattered doorway, they crept close together for a whispered parley.

"So far so good," murmured Frank.

"Luck's been with us," agreed Bert.

"We can stand a whole lot of luck in this business," whispered Tom.

"It's a long, long way yet to our own lines," said Billy. "We haven't got more than a couple of blocks away from our old hangout, and there's no telling how much further it is before we strike the open country."

Just then a stone toppled from a wall and fell with a crash only a few feet away. In their tense state of alertness the unexpected sound made them jump.

"Just as well we weren't under that," remarked Frank, with a sigh of relief.

"Let's hope it won't bring some German sentry along to see what's making the racket," responded Bart.

"Just what it is doing," whispered Tom, as he heard a step

approaching. "Quick, fellows, get further back and lie down flat."

They almost ceased to breathe as a dim form passed by so close that they could almost have reached out and touched him. But the dust still rising from the shattered stone convinced the visitor that nature and not man was responsible for the disturbance, and, with a grunt of satisfaction that it was nothing worse, the sentry returned to his former post.

But the promptness with which he had appeared warned the fugitives that the town, desolate as it was, was still under guard, and they redoubled their precautions. However dangerous it might be, they must go on. The moon would rise before long, and they must make the most of the pitchy darkness that still prevailed.

Listening with all their ears and straining their eyes until they ached, they made their way through the littered streets until they realized from their frequent encounters with bush and hedge that they were getting into the open country.

Huddled close in a thicket, they consulted the radio compass that Frank drew from his pocket. That gave them the general direction in which they must go. They knew that in general their course led toward the west, but, as they could not tell what changes had taken place in the position of the armies as the result of the two days' fighting, they had no idea of how long it might take them to reach the American lines.

They got their bearings due west and set off. They were making fair progress when they were startled by hearing the clatter of hoofs a little ahead of them.

"Listen!" hissed Bart.

"It's a cavalry troop," whispered Frank, as he flattened himself behind a bush, an example that was promptly followed by the others.

"Troop!" growled Tom. "It sounds more like a brigade."

"Uhlans, probably," conjectured Billy.

They peered through the bushes at the broad road not more than twenty feet away.

At that moment the moon showed a slender rim above the horizon and threaded the darkness with a faint shimmer of light.

Along the road came a force of cavalry. The guttural voices of the riders told the concealed watchers that they belonged to the enemy. In the dim light they could see the steam that rose from the horses' flanks.

Those days had been the first for a long time that cavalry could be used on the western front. Trench fighting had put that arm of the service almost wholly out of action. But the fact that the Allies had followed up their tank attack with cavalry had brought forth a German response of the same nature.

There was no sign of elation among the riders, and the boys drew pleasure from that. A dejected air prevailed, as though the Uhlans had had the worst of it.

"Guess they've had the hot end of the poker," whispered Bart.

"Looks like it," replied Frank.

Something just then frightened one of the horses, and he reared and plunged into the bushes at the side of the road. The boys had all they could do to scramble out of reach of the iron-shod hoofs. The rider was almost unhorsed, but managed to retain his seat and quiet his trembling mount.

By the time he had done this, the troopers had almost passed. The boys were rejoicing at this, but their exultation changed to uneasiness when the soldier who had had so much trouble rode up to an officer and began to talk volubly, at the same time pointing toward the bushes.

"Here's where I see trouble coming," muttered Tom.

"He's on to us," agreed Bart.

"He must have seen us when we got out of his way," said Frank. "Let's get out of here, quick."

But this was not to be done so easily, for even as he spoke the officer rapped out a command and a group of twenty horsemen began to spread out and surround the place where the Army boys were crouching.

To remain there would be fatal, for it was only a matter of a few minutes before that ring would close upon them with a grip of iron. At all hazards they must break through.

"Stick together, fellows," murmured Frank. "Get your rifles ready. We can't miss at this distance. When I say the word, give them a volley and make a break for the road. It's our only chance, for they'd surely round us up in these bushes."

"We're with you, boy," replied Bart, and the little party crouched lower with their fingers on trigger.

Frank waited until the nearest horsemen were not more than ten feet away. Then he sprang to his feet with a shout.

"Fire!" he cried, and a stream of flame leaped from the bushes.

Two of the riders threw up their hands and pitched from their saddles. A third seized with his left hand the rein that dropped from his right. There was a moment of confusion, and Frank and his comrades took instant advantage of it.

With a rush they reached the road and tore down it for dear life, while behind them thundered the Uhlans in hot pursuit!

CHAPTER XVII

THE BROKEN BRIDGE

The Army boys had no idea where the road led to. It might be to the American lines or to the German lines. But they knew that certain death was behind them and possible life in front of them, and they ran as though their feet had wings.

But swift as they were, the horses were of course swifter, and before long they knew that their pursuers were gaining.

"Throw away your rifles," panted Frank. "We'll still have our knives and grenades."

They threw the heavy rifles aside, and, relieved of their weight, they bounded ahead with renewed speed.

For a short time their desperate efforts held their pursuers even, but soon the gap again began to close.

At a turn of the road they halted, gasping for breath.

"Give them the grenades," ordered Frank, getting his own ready. "They won't be expecting them and it may upset them. Throw yours at the same time I do mine."

They waited until the horsemen were within fifty feet. Then four stalwart arms hurled the grenades against the front ranks.

There was a tremendous explosion as the shells all seemed to go off at the same instant, and the first rank of horsemen went down in a heap.

Those behind drew their beasts back on their haunches so as not to override their fellows, and in that moment another volley came among them with deadly effect.

Without waiting any longer, the boys renewed their flight. They knew that the Germans would be mad with rage at their check by so small a force, and they were not foolish enough to believe for a moment that the chase would be abandoned.

But a new exultation was in their hearts as they ran. They might be killed, but they would at least have sold their lives dearly. There would be little that the Uhlans would have to boast of in their story of that night's work.

Their breath came in short gasps and their laboring lungs felt as though they were ready to burst. Frank, a little in the van, reached out a warning hand and they slowed up.

"We'll make faster time if we give ourselves a minute's rest," he panted. "When we start in again we'll have our second wind. They haven't got out of that mix-up yet. Besides, they'll come on more cautiously now. They won't know how many grenades we have left."

"I haven't any," gasped Tom.

Billy was too far gone to speak, but he drew his last grenade from his sack. Bart and Frank also were down to their last one, for the work on the previous day had almost used up the stock with which they had started out. They had a chance for one last throw, and then if it came to a hand to hand fight they had nothing to rely on but their knives.

They rested for a minute or two, and then again upon the wind came the sound of hurrying hoofs.

Instinctively the boys reached out and grasped one another's hands. There was no need for words. They knew what it meant. To some of them this might prove the last lap of the last race they would ever run.

On came their pursuers, and the boys, summoning up every ounce of strength they possessed, set out at the pace of hunted deer.

Not two minutes had elapsed before their feet struck the boards of a bridge. Below they saw the gleam of the moon in the dark water that ran beneath.

They took heart at the sight and put on a new burst of speed. Who knew but what the American troops were camped on the further side?

Twenty feet further they stopped abruptly. The bridge was broken. The boards had been torn up, though the shattered timbers of the sides projected a few feet further over the current. But fully a hundred feet of black water stretched between them and the farther shore.

They stopped, panting and perplexed. And just at that moment they heard the hoofs of horses on the wood of the bridge.

They were trapped. To turn back was certain captivity or

death. To plunge into that black current might also mean death. Their choice was made on the instant.

"Over we go, boys!" shouted Frank, throwing off his coat. "But we mustn't waste those last grenades. Let them have them."

They turned and threw, and without waiting to see the result dived headforemost into the stream. The roar of the explosion was in their ears as they struck the water.

They were all good swimmers, and when they came to the surface they found themselves within a few feet of each other.

"To the other bank, fellows!" exclaimed Frank, as he shook the water from his eyes. "And keep as low in the water as you can. They'll send a volley after us."

They struck out lustily for the farther shore while, as Frank had predicted, bullets zipped around them. But in the darkness their foes could take no aim and they reached the shore unscathed.

The bank was steep, with long reeds growing down to the water's edge. The fugitives grasped these and rested before they attempted to climb the bank.

"I'm all in," gasped Tom.

Frank reached out a supporting hand.

"I guess we all are," he replied. "It's lucky this river isn't wider. But we're safe now."

"I don't know about that," said Bart. "Listen!"

There was a tramp of many feet upon the bank.

"They've heard the shooting," whispered Billy. "If it's our boys we're all right. If it isn't—"

The sentence was never finished. Above the bank they saw a crowd of helmeted figures. A light was flashed into their faces, nearly blinding them, and a hoarse voice cried:

"*Wer da!*"

A score of hands reached down and grasped them. Unarmed, dripping, utterly exhausted, they found themselves in the hands of the soldiers of the Kaiser!

CHAPTER XVIII

RESCUE FROM THE SKY

With a file of soldiers on either side of them, the four boys were marched off to a dugout near at hand. Here a German outpost had been stationed to watch the river bank. It was not a large command, and the lieutenant in charge, being unable to speak English and having no interpreter at hand, after a few brusque attempts to question them gave it up. Then, after having had them searched, he committed them to the custody of a non-commissioned officer with directions that they were to be fed and sent to headquarters in the morning. They ate ravenously, and, not being permitted to talk to each other, found solace in sorely needed sleep.

When taken before the German officers, the friends were forced to undergo a strict and searching examination. Their questioners tried in every way, with pleadings alternating with threats, to get them to divulge information that might be useful to them, but in vain. The four Americans were absolutely uncommunicative, and at last the German who had been doing most of the questioning was forced to acknowledge defeat.

"*Donnerwetter!*" he growled. "Yankee pigs! It must be that they are so stupid that they do not know anything to tell.

What do you think, Herr Lieutenant?" turning to one of his officers.

"I think it more likely that they are just obstinate, sir, like those cursed English," replied the officer addressed. "But perhaps a few months in a prison camp will incline them to answer more quickly when a German speaks to them." This was accompanied by a cruel smile, whose significance was hot lost on the Americans. The captain glared at them, but as they did not seem to weaken perceptibly, even under his high displeasure, he grumbled finally:

"Well, take them away, and we'll see how they act after a taste of prison life." As their guards were about to take them from the room, he continued, menacingly: "Remember, you Yankees, that the sooner you tell me what I want to know, the easier it will be for you. And in the end we'll make you talk. It is not well to oppose Germany's will too far."

But as the prisoners did not appear greatly frightened by these threats, the commander at last ordered the sergeant in charge to take the prisoners away, and turned again to his desk.

In spite of the critical situation in which they found themselves, Bart could not resist a surreptitious wink at his companions as they passed through the doorway, which was returned in kind by his graceless companions. But, although they had had the satisfaction of balking the German officers, they were not long in appreciating the discomforts of their present situation. When they reached the temporary prison camp, they were herded into a large tent, already overcrowded with French, English, and a few American prisoners. Soon after their arrival food was served out, although it hardly seemed worthy of the name. Watery soup, made by boiling turnips in water, and a small chunk of some tasteless substance supposed to be bread, constituted the meal. The boys, fresh from the wholesome and abundant food furnished by Uncle Sam, found it absolutely uneatable, and gave away their portions to some of the other prisoners, who appeared glad to get it.

"Wait until you've been here a few days," said one lanky Englishman, with a ghastly smile, "you'll get so thoroughly famished that you'll be able to go even that stuff," and he made a wry face.

"Perhaps so, if we can't find some way to get out," said Frank.

"Not as easy as it sounds," said the Englishman. "Although it has been done, of course. But a lot more have been shot trying it than have ever got away."

"Might as well get shot as die of starvation," remarked Tom.

This opinion evidently appealed to Tom's comrades, who looked significantly at him. From that look each knew that the others were ready to risk everything to gain their freedom. The Englishman, however, seemed unconvinced, and presently left them.

As night came on, they cast about for some place to sleep, but met with little success. The only place to lie was on the ground, but by that time the four friends were so tired that sleep, even under any hardship, was desirable. They finally settled down in a corner that appeared a little less crowded than the rest. However, before going to sleep they tried to formulate some plan of escape, but with indifferent success.

"About all we can do," said Bart finally, "is to hold ourselves in readiness to make use of the first chance of escape that comes along. And if these Germans are all as stupid as the ones we've seen so far, it oughtn't to be very difficult."

"Well, when the chance comes, we won't let any grass grow under our feet, that's certain," said Frank. "But now, I'm dog-tired, and I'm going to see if I can't get a little sleep. And what's more, I'd advise you fellows to do the same."

"He who sleeps, dines," quoted Tom, with a somewhat rueful grin. "I hope there's more in that old saying than there is in most of them."

"Right you are," said Bart, "but something seems to tell me I'm going to be hungry in the morning, just the same."

Bart was right. After a restless night, the boys woke with ravenous appetites, and managed to eat most of the unpalatable fare that was passed around. Not long after this they saw the sergeant who had had charge of them the previous day picking his way through the crowd, evidently looking for some particular object. At last he caught sight of the Americans, and immediately headed toward them.

"Come," he commanded, roughly, in his halting English. "Orders have come for your removal."

"Where to?" inquired Frank. "Silence! Do as you are told, and ask no questions!" commanded the German.

"For two cents I'd jump on him and choke the dog's life out of him!" muttered Tom, but his friends laid restraining hands on him.

"Nothing doing, Tom," warned Billy. "We'd be playing against stacked cards in a game like that. Take it easy now, and maybe our chance will come later."

Meanwhile the sergeant had started off, and the friends had no choice but to follow him. He led them out of the tent, where a squad of soldiers was lined up. At a nod from the sergeant, these surrounded the boys, and at a curt word of command they all started off.

They were soon outside the confines of the camp, and marching along what had once been a perfect road, but was now badly broken up by the combined effects of shellfire and heavy trucking. The soldiers talked among themselves in low gutturals, and the boys, by piecing together words that they caught here and there, gathered that they were being taken to some higher official for further questioning.

"You see," said Billy, "they know we were inside their lines a considerable time before they caught us, and so they are paying particular attention to us. I guess they think we may know more than we've told them so far." This with a wink at his friends.

"We sure have told them a lot," put in Bart, grinning. "And, just to be perfectly fair, I suggest that we tell the next Boche who questions us just as much as we told the last one."

"Fair enough," agreed Tom. "No favoritism has always been my motto."

"No talking among the prisoners," commanded the sergeant, threateningly, and the four friends, having said about all they wanted to say, anyway, relapsed into silence.

For several miles the little group plodded along, often meeting detachments of German infantry, who scowled sullenly at the Americans as they passed.

The boys were far from happy, in spite of the light-hearted

attitude they presented to their captors. They all knew that if they could not effect an escape their chance for life was small, as, on account of their having been inside the German lines so long before being captured, the Huns would seize the opportunity of calling them spies, and mete out the quick end that is accorded to such. They were walking along, each one immersed in his own gloomy thoughts, when suddenly a sound from above caused them to look quickly up toward the blue sky.

What they saw caused their hearts to beat faster and hope to spring up again in their breasts. For, skilled as they were in such matters, they recognized the airplane up above, whose roaring exhaust had first attracted their attention, as one of the Allied type.

It was coming toward them at high speed, flying low, and as it rapidly neared them the four friends, forgetting their German captors, waved their hands wildly to the pilot, whom they could see, as the aeroplane came closer, peering down over the side of the body. The Germans, on their part, were so terrified by the approach of this huge enemy machine, that they seemed to forget all about their prisoners, and in fact about everything except their individual safety. With wild yells of terror they scattered this way and that, all except the sergeant. He, seeing his men running in every direction, snarled out a curse, and whipped out his automatic pistol.

"I'll do for you Yankees, anyway, he hissed," and leveled the pistol at them. But even as his finger trembled on the trigger, Frank's fist, with the force of a sledgehammer, came with a crashing impact against the point of the German's jaw, and the Hun went down, his pistol exploding harmlessly toward the sky. Frank, with the light of battle in his eye, seized the fallen man's weapon and looked around for the other Germans. But by this time they had all gotten out of effective pistol range, and after emptying the weapon in the direction of the fleeing figures, Frank and the others turned their attention to the aeroplane, which by now was manoeuvring for a landing.

The airship came down in great spirals, and finally took the ground with hardly a jar, running along a hundred feet or so and then coming to a halt.

As the boys started running toward it, Tom ejaculated: "Say, fellows, my eyes may be playing me tricks, but if that isn't Dick Lever at the wheel you can call me a German!"

"I think it is Dick, myself," agreed Frank. "And if this isn't a case of the 'friend in need,' I miss my guess."

It was indeed as they thought. The pilot was an old friend of theirs, but one whom they had not seen for some time. Now, as they raced toward the airplane, he in turn recognized them, and raised a delirious shout of joy.

"Tumble into this bus just as fast as you can, fellows," he cried, "we've got to get out of this mighty quick. You can explain the mystery of your being here after we get started."

"But can you carry the whole bunch of us?" asked Billy.

"Easily," replied one of the two observers, who had not spoken up to now. "We've just dropped our load of bombs on a few German supply depots, and now we're running back light."

"All right, then," said Billy, "in we go!" And, suiting the action to the word, the four friends swarmed into the airplane, filling the cramped passenger carrying space to overflowing. Meantime, the Germans, having found cover, had opened up a brisk rifle fire against the aeroplane, and bullets began to sing through the framework. One of the observers leaped to the ground, gave the propeller a vigorous twist, and as the motor began to roar clambered aboard as the big plane started over the rough ground, bumping and jolting, but rapidly gaining speed. The Germans broke from their shelter in pursuit, firing wildly as they ran, but although some of their shots came close, none came near enough to do any real damage. In a few seconds, in answer to a quick movement from Dick Lever, the big bombing machine left the ground, and amid a parting rain of bullets from the Germans, started to ascend in long, sweeping spirals.

The friends were about to congratulate themselves on their safe escape, when suddenly one of the observers, who had been scanning the horizon closely, pointed behind them, and exclaimed:

"Just as I thought! Those two Boche planes that we saw getting ready to come after us just after we dropped our last bomb are coming up fast. Look!"

All twisted about, and saw that it was as the observer had said. High up in the sky two swift, darting objects were coming in pursuit. The American machine was built more for carrying capacity than for speed, and in addition was heavily loaded. Every advantage was with the swift German machines. Their pilots no doubt realized this, for now they headed directly for the Americans, descending in a long slant that gave them tremendous speed.

"All right," said Lever, coolly, "if they're going to come down, it may be a good idea for us to go up," and, suiting the action to the word, he elevated the nose of the big plane skyward, and they started to climb steeply. The American machine was equipped with a tremendously powerful motor, and this, combined with its great wing spread, enabled it to climb with great rapidity, in spite of the heavy load it was carrying. The Germans had not counted on this, and the result was that they miscalculated their distances, passing beneath the American flyer instead of above it, as they had intended. They both turned quickly and started to climb, but by this time the American aviators had trained their two machine guns on the Germans, and opened fire.

At first this seemed to have little effect, and the Germans ascended rapidly, while their machine gun operators, although as yet unable to use their deadly weapons, sent a hail of revolver bullets whistling through the wings and rigging of the American machine. But now the concentrated fire from the American machine was beginning to have effect. One of the German planes hesitated, quivered, and suddenly its right wing, with its wire stays severed by the machine gun bullets, crumpled up. The crippled aeroplane staggered wildly, suddenly turned on its right side, and pitched steeply downward.

The boys in the American airplane gazed at each other with white faces, but they had little time to devote to thoughts of the fallen, for by now the remaining German machine was on a level with them, and its machine gunner opened fire. The Americans, crouching low to avoid the murderous stream of bullets, returned the fire from both their machine guns, with a deadliness of purpose and aim for which the German was no match. Suddenly a tiny flame appeared in the body of the German machine, grew with lightning rapidity, and in a few seconds one side of the machine was enveloped in leaping yellow flames.

"Punctured the gas tank!" exulted Lever. "They're done for now."

And he was right. The machine gun fire from both fighting planes died out, and the boys could see the Germans vainly trying to beat out the hungry flames. Their efforts were useless, however, and in a few seconds the German machine, a roaring mass of flame and black smoke, dropped downward as swiftly as a stone. As it went, the boys saw two figures hurl themselves out into space, and then everything was hidden in a haze of billowy smoke.

"That's awful!" exclaimed Tom, drawing in his breath with a great sigh, while all relaxed from the terrible tension they had been under.

"Awful, yes," said Dick Lever. "But it's only what they would have done to us if they had been able. Instead of 'live and let live,' it's 'kill or get killed' in this game."

Frank nodded his head gloomily, but none of the boys felt like talking then, and sat silent as their pilot got his bearings and then straightened out swiftly in the direction of the American lines.

With the roar of the motor in their ears and the rush of wind past their faces, much of the horror of the deadly air battle was swept from their minds, and they began to enjoy the exhilaration of their first flight. The distant earth streamed rapidly by, like a swiftly flowing river, and a wonderful panorama was spread out below them. It was an exceptionally clear day, and they could see for many miles in every direction. Below them, groups of gray clad figures, after a glance in the direction of the soaring monster overhead, broke for cover, or, shaking impotent fists, trudged stolidly onward, contemptuous of one more danger among the many that daily surrounded them.

"No prison camp for us this time," exulted Frank, as he

looked down at his enemies.

"We wouldn't have been in a prison camp long," declared Tom. "Those fellows had picked us out for a firing squad. They were going to get all they could out of us, and then about six feet of earth would have been our size."

"I'll bet that sergeant's jaw aches yet from the clip that Frank handed him," chuckled Billy happily.

"I skinned my knuckles," said Frank, looking at them ruefully.

"Never mind," laughed Bart. "You never hurt them in a better cause."

"We can't be far from the lines now," shouted Frank, in Dick's ear.

"Pretty close," responded the aviator. "We ought to be down fifteen minutes from now."

And his estimate proved very nearly correct. Soon the boys of the old Thirty-seventh could recognize the familiar landmarks of their own encampment, and, with one impulse, they gave three rousing cheers.

CHAPTER XIX

PUTTING ONE OVER

It was a beautiful landing that Dick Lever made at the aviation camp, his great machine sailing down like a swan and landing so lightly that it would scarcely have broken a pane of glass.

"Dick, you're a wonder!" exclaimed Frank, as he stepped out of the machine.

"The way you put it all over the Boche planes shows that," chimed in Bart with equal enthusiasm.

"I don't wonder they say you're an 'ace,'" added Billy.

"If all aviators had your class, the Hun flyers wouldn't have a chance on earth—I mean in the sky," said Tom.

"Oh, it's all a matter of practice," said Dick modestly, although it was plain to be seen that their heartfelt appreciation pleased him. "It's as easy as running an automobile when you know how. Well, so long, fellows. I've got to make my report," and with a gay wave of the hand he left them and made his way to aviation headquarters.

"Say, how does it feel to be a free man once more?" cried Frank jubilantly, as they sought out their regiment.

"I can't believe yet that it's anything but a dream." replied Bart with deep feeling, as he looked around at the friendly faces and familiar surroundings that he had feared for a time he would never see again.

"And look at that flag!" cried Billy as he saw Old Glory flying from one of the officers' pavilions. Like a flash their hats came off and they saluted the glorious flag that meant to them everything in life.

They passed the tanks, and Will Stone, who was "grooming his pet," looked at them for a moment as though he could not believe his eyes. Then he rushed toward them and nearly shook their hands off.

"By all that is lucky!" he cried. "I was afraid I was never going to see you fellows again. Where did you drop from?"

"From the sky," laughed Frank.

"Some little angels, you see," chuckled Billy. Then seeing Stone's puzzled look he added: "The Huns had got their hooks on us when Dick Lever came along in his plane, gave them a few little leaden missives, picked us up and landed us here, right side up with care."

Stone's eyes kindled as he heard their story, and his enthusiasm over Lever's feat was as great as their own.

"But how did we make out in the big drive?" asked Frank. "We kept hoping all the time that you fellows would be along and nab us before the Boches did."

"We've had a big victory," explained Stone. "We put the Hindenburg line on the blink by that smash at his center, and he's had to draw in his wings on both sides. It's one of the biggest things that's been done on the western front, and the Heinies will have a hard time explaining it in Berlin."

"That's bully!" exclaimed Frank.

"That town you fellows were hiding in didn't come into our general plan," went on Stone, "and that's the reason you had to fight your way out all by your lonesome."

"It was some little fight, all right," remarked Tom.

"And we certainly gave those Uhlans a run for their money," laughed Billy.

"Lucky they didn't get hold of you," said Stone. "It would have been curtains for the whole bunch. They must have been wild at the lacing you handed them."

"I guess they were rather peeved," grinned Bart.

"I'm sorry I had to throw away my rifle, though," mourned Tom.

"Tom would find something to grouch about if he were in heaven," laughed Frank.

They talked for a few minutes longer and then went on, as they were eager to be once more with their comrades of the old Thirty-seventh.

And what a greeting they had when they walked into their old command! They were pounded and mauled in wild enthusiasm, for they were prime favorites in the regiment and had been sadly given up as dead or captured.

They had to tell again and again the story of their adventures, and it was only by main force that they tore themselves away from their rejoicing mates long enough to report themselves to their officers as present for duty.

Their captain was as delighted as his men at their safe return, although his satisfaction was expressed in less boisterous fashion. He commended warmly the gallant fight they had put up with the Uhlans, and he was visibly startled as his eye glanced over the German report that had been captured by Frank when it fluttered down into the cellar.

"This must go to headquarters at once!" he exclaimed. "It is a matter of the utmost importance. You men have deserved the thanks of the army," he continued, "and I am proud that you are members of my command."

They made their way back to their company with their leader's praise ringing in their ears and warming their hearts. But they had scarcely got out of the captain's presence before his chums pounced upon Frank with the liveliest curiosity.

"How did you keep that paper when the Germans searched you?" asked Tom.

"Where did you hide it?" demanded Billy.

"I never knew you were a sleight of hand performer," added Bart.

"Easy there, fellows," laughed Frank, enjoying their mystification. "It was the simplest thing in the world. While you fellows were sleeping in the cellar I just loosened the sole of my shoe and slipped the paper in between the sole and the upper and nailed the sole up again. The Heinies didn't get next to it, and that's where I had luck. I'm mighty glad they didn't, for the cap seems to think there's something in it that's worth while."

"Foxy stunt," approved Tom.

"Some wise boy!" exclaimed Billy, giving his chum a slap on the shoulder that made him wince.

"You're all there when it comes to the gray matter, old man," was Bart's tribute.

A day later, part of their reward came in a week's furlough that was granted them for "specially gallant conduct," as the order of the day expressed it. The rest was welcome, for it was the first they had had since they had landed on French soil, and they had been under a strain of hard work and harder fighting that had taxed even their strong vitality to the utmost.

And that week stood out forever in their memory like an oasis in a desert. They spent it in a little French town miles away from the firing line and even beyond the sound of the guns. They fished and swam and loafed and slept as though there was no such thing as war in the world. No reveille to wake them in the morning, no taps to send them to their beds at night. For the first time in months they were their own masters, and they enjoyed their brief liberty to the full.

Yet even here in this "little bit of heaven" as Tom expressed it, they could not be wholly free from war's reminder.

They were sprawling one day outside their cottage when an officer came along, gorgeous in epaulets and gold lace.

"See who's coming!" exclaimed Tom peevishly. "Now we'll have to get up and salute."

"I suppose so," said Billy reluctantly.

"Can't we pretend, we don't see him?" yawned Bart sleepily, clutching at a straw of hope.

"Not a chance in the world," declared Frank. "He's looking right at us."

They stood up as the officer approached and saluted respectfully. He returned the salute snappishly and glared at them sternly.

"Get in line there," he commanded. "Smart now. Eyes ahead."

They resented his tone, but obeyed with military promptness.

"Present arms."

They hesitated and looked at each other.

"Present arms," I said.

"If you please, sir," said Bart, "we have no guns."

"I know it," snapped the officer. "Go through the motions."

So without a word they did as directed.

"Shoulder arms."

They did so.

"Forward! March!"

He set off in front with a military stride and they followed.

"I feel like a fool," whispered Bart to Frank.

"Same here," was the reply. "What does he mean by it?"

"Wants to show his authority, I reckon," muttered Bart.

Tom and Billy said nothing, but there were scowls on their faces that spoke for them.

They had marched for perhaps half a mile, when at a cross roads two men appeared who were evidently looking for some one. Their eyes lighted up when they saw the officer and they came straight toward him. He saw them coming, and throwing his dignity to the wind started to run, but they were quicker than he and grasped him by the collar.

"Come back to the asylum," one of them growled. "We've had lots of trouble to find you."

The boys stood rooted to the spot.

"You see," explained one of the men, touching his forehead significantly, "he's a grocer that's got the military bug. He thinks he's Napoleon. Come along, Napoleon."

And "Napoleon" meekly obeyed.

CHAPTER XX

SUSPICION

To paint the emotions that chased themselves over the features of the four boys would have taxed the ability of an artist. For a moment no one of them cared to look into the eyes of the others.

Tom was the first to act. He grabbed his cap in his hands, kneaded it into a ball, threw it on the ground and jumped up and down on it.

The others looked at his scowling face and the sight was too much for them. They threw themselves on the ground in convulsions of laughter. They howled. They roared. They rolled over and over, until Tom himself caught the contagion and joined in with the rest. It was a long time before any one of them was able to speak.

"Stung!" choked Bart, while tears of merriment rolled down his cheeks.

"Forward! March!" gurgled Billy. "Pound me on the back, you fellows, or I'll have a fit."

"A grocer! Napoleon!" roared Frank. "Shades of Austerlitz

and Waterloo!"

"And we fell for it!" yelled Tom. "Think of it, fellows! By the great horn spoon! We fell for it!"

They got themselves under control at last, though not without many interruptions, for again and again one of them would start to speak and go off into a peal of laughter.

"I'm as weak as a rag," gulped Billy. "I haven't laughed like this in all my life."

"It would make a hit in vaudeville," chuckled Bart. "Think of us sillies stalking along and going through shadow motions for a nut like that. We're squirrel food, all right."

"Well, after all what could we do?" defended Frank. "We're not mind readers."

"Not even of a scrambled mind like that," interposed Billy.

"And we couldn't tell that he wasn't an officer," went on Frank, not heeding the interruption. "His uniform seemed to be all right, although a bit gaudy."

"That gives us a way out," said Bart. "We can say that we followed the uniform, not the man, and let it go at that. But, oh, boy! if the fellows of our regiment had seen us trotting along behind that lunatic, maybe they wouldn't make our life a burden."

"We'd never have heard the last of it," agreed Tom. "But what they don't know won't hurt them, and it's a safe bet that none of us will ever let out a squeak."

"It's lucky there wasn't any moving picture man handy,"

laughed Frank. "He'd have had a film that would put all the rest out of business. But now let's get back to the cottage after this unfortunate hike of ours."

"Say," put in Bart, as a new thought struck him, "do you think those keepers could have caught on?"

"I don't think they tumbled," Billy reassured them. "They were too intent on catching Napoleon to think of anything else."

"Poor Napoleon," chuckled Frank. "I suppose he's back on St. Helena by this time."

"Well, there's one comfort, anyway," declared Tom. "He doesn't know that he put anything over on us. If he hasn't forgotten us altogether he thinks we're part of the Old Guard."

"They say a philosopher is one who can grin when the laugh is on himself," laughed Billy. "If that's so we're dandy philosophers."

All too soon that pleasant week was over, and the boys, refreshed and rested, went away, though with many a backward glance, to the stern work where they had already won their spurs and made their mark.

They started in on their work again with renewed zest and with quickened energy, for a battle was impending and they were anxious to take their part in driving back the Hun.

They saw Rabig frequently, and though they all disliked him heartily, he was still a soldier like themselves in the service of Uncle Sam, and they strove to disguise their feeling for the good of the common cause.

"He's a bad egg, all right," declared Tom, who stuck obstinately to his belief that Rabig had had some part in the escape of the German corporal, "but as long as we can't prove it, we'll have to give him a little more rope. But sooner or later he'll come to the end of that rope, and don't you forget it!"

Nick had come out of the court-martial that investigated the escape, not with flying colors, but with bedraggled feathers. The cut on his head had proved so slight as to arouse suspicion that it might have been self-inflicted. Still the motive for this did not seem adequate, and the upshot of the inquiry was that Rabig was confined a few days in the guardhouse and then restored to duty. But in the private books of the officers there was a black mark against him, and all of them would have been better pleased not to have had him in the regiment.

"Oh, well, don't let's talk about him," Frank summed up a discussion about the bully. "The whole subject leaves a bad taste in my mouth. I only hope he's the only rotten apple in the barrel."

"That's just the trouble'," replied Tom. "If that rotten apple isn't taken out of the barrel a good many more may be spoiled in less than no time."

"Sure enough," agreed Bart. "But I guess there isn't much danger in this case. If Nick had lots of friends that he might influence it might be different, but you notice that the fellows leave him to flock by himself."

"He's about as popular as the hives in summertime for a fact," commented Tom. "He'd be a mighty sight more at home if he were in the trenches on the other side."

"Maybe so," admitted Frank.

"What are you fellows chinning about?" broke in a familiar voice, and they turned to see Dick Lever regarding them with a friendly grin.

"Hello, Dick," came from them all at once in a roar of welcome, for it was the first time they had seen him since he had rescued them from their German captors, and their feelings toward him were of the warmest nature.

"Where have you been keeping yourself?" asked Frank. "We've been looking for you to drop in and see us for a long time past."

"As a matter of fact, I did get down this way about a week ago," replied Dick, as he tried to shake hands with all four at once, "but the whole bunch of you were off on furlough."

"Sorry we missed you," said Frank. "Yes, we did get a few days off, and it didn't do us a bit of harm. We've all come back feeling the best ever."

"Ready to take another crack at the Huns, eh?" grinned Dick. "Some fellows never know when they have enough."

"You needn't talk," laughed Bart. "I'll bet you've been popping away at them every day since we saw you last."

"Oh, they've kept me pretty busy," said Dick carelessly. "The Hun flyers are getting pretty sassy just now, and we have to keep working hard to drive them back."

"I've noticed more of them flying over our lines than usual in the last day or two," remarked Billy.

"Say," broke in Tom, "this is sure our lucky day. Here comes Will Stone."

"We sure are lucky when two of the best fellows in the world drop in on us at the same time," said Frank, as he and his mates greeted the bronzed tank operator. "I don't know whether you two fellows know each other, but if you don't you've both lost something."

"Oh, we're not altogether strangers," smiled Stone, as he and Dick shook hands heartily. "Many a time I've seen his plane flying overhead, and it's made me feel rather comfortable to know that he was on the job, and that no Boche flyer would have a chance to drop something that would put Jumbo out of commission."

"It would have to be some bomb that would make junk of that big car of yours," said Dick. "I was flying pretty low the day we smashed the Boche lines and I saw the way Jumbo snapped those wires as though they were so many threads. That tank's a wonder and no mistake."

They were having such a good time and the time flew so rapidly that they were startled when the bugle blew and they were compelled to go to their respective quarters.

A few nights after his return Frank was assigned to sentry duty on an important post on the front trenches. His beat terminated at a point where he could see a little shack that stood on the side of a hill.

Standing as it did in the battle zone; it had become little more than a ruin. Most of the thatched roof had been shot away, one side had gone altogether, and the other three sides leaned crazily toward each other.

It was a little after midnight when Frank thought he saw a gleam of light either in the cabin or close by it. It was very faint, scarcely more than the glimmer of a firefly, and it vanished instantly.

Still, it had been there. Cautiously, avoiding every twig with the stealth of an Indian, Frank crept toward the hut.

CHAPTER XXI

A FAMILIAR VOICE

As Frank neared the cabin he redoubled his precautions, and it was here that his scout training stood him in good stead.

When he was within twenty feet he went down flat on the earth and wormed his way to one of the sides that had been left standing. He placed his ear against a board and listened intently.

But not a sound rewarded him. The deepest silence reigned.

For a moment he was tempted to believe that his eyes had played a trick on him. But they had seldom done this and he had learned to trust them.

The light could not have come from a firefly, for it was too late in the season for them. What then had caused it?

He worked his way around to the shattered doorway and inch by inch lifted his head until his eyes were on a level with the floor. Quickly they swept the room, which was so small that the faint light that came from the stars enabled him to see that it was empty.

When he was fully assured of this, he crept into the room and with his fingers explored every inch of the floor. The apartment was so small that this was not much of a task, and before long his hand came in contact with a match. It had been lighted and the softness of the charred end told him that this had been done recently.

This then was the "firefly"!

He continued his search with renewed caution and soon found a cartridge. He knew from the feel of it that it was of the kind used in the rifles with which the American troops were equipped. It was still warm, as though it had been recently in a belt close to a man's body.

But what was a man doing in that lonely spot at that hour of the night?

Was he a prowling spy from the German camp who had made a daring incursion into the American lines?

He must solve the mystery. With every faculty at its highest pitch, he moved out into the open.

A slight rustling in the forest near by fell on his ears. It might have been made by some woodland creature, but to his strained senses every sound, however slight, suggested a possible clue.

He listened intently and heard it again, but this time it was a trifle louder than before.

He rose to his feet and with catlike tread moved in the direction of the sound. As he drew hearer he heard it more plainly. And now his patience was rewarded, for he distinctly heard the low tone of a human voice.

And if it was a human voice it must of necessity be an enemy voice, for no friend of his or of Uncle Sam's could be in that place at that hour on a legitimate errand.

A moment later he detected another voice in a different key yet pitched hardly above a whisper. So it was a conference! A conference of whom and about what?

He crept still farther forward.

Right before him stretched a little glade full of small trees and undergrowth with a scarcely visible path leading downward.

To press too far between the bushes would have inevitably betrayed him. He halted with his rifle ready for action and listened.

The conversation seemed to be an earnest one and in their earnestness the conferees at times forgot caution, for, as one of the men raised his voice in expostulation, Frank could note that he was talking German. But it was not that which made him start suddenly and clutch his rifle more tightly.

He had heard that voice before.

Where and when?

He cudgeled his brain and then it came to him.

It was Nick Rabig's voice!

That is, he thought it was. But at that distance he could not be perfectly sure. At any rate it was time to act.

With a bound he leaped forward.

"Halt!" he cried. "Halt or I fire."

There were startled exclamations from both men, and then a prodigious scrambling in the bushes as they tried to escape.

Bang! went Frank's rifle, and there was a scream followed by a heavy fall.

Frank rushed forward, but caught his foot in a tangled root and fell. His gun flew from his hand and his head came in contact with a stump. The jagged edges cut a gash in his forehead, and for a moment he was utterly dazed.

He strove desperately to retain his senses and in a minute or two his brain ceased to whirl. He staggered drunkenly to his rifle and picked it up. And at this moment there was a sound of hurrying feet, and Wilson, the corporal of the guard, came running up, accompanied by Fred Anderson who had been on duty near by.

"What is it, Sheldon?" asked the corporal "What were you shooting at?"

Frank tried to speak, but his tongue was thick and the words would not come."

"He's wounded!" exclaimed Anderson, as he saw with alarm the blood flowing freely from Frank's forehead.

They deftly bound up his head, and by this time Frank had found his voice.

"It's nothing," he managed to say. "I fell and cut my head. It's only a scratch. I heard two men talking German here in the bushes and I started in to get them. They wouldn't stop when I ordered them to, and I fired, I don't know whether I got them or not."

"We'll see," said the corporal, and led the way into the bushes while Frank and Fred followed close on his heels.

From one side to the other the corporal flashed his light, and before long he uttered an exclamation.

"You got one of them anyway," he said, as the light fell on the dead body of a German whose uniform showed that he belonged to the Eighth Bavarian Regiment, which they knew was stationed opposite them at that part of the line.

The corporal blew his whistle and other men of his squad came running in answer to the call. He ordered them to carry the body into camp where it could be searched for papers. Then he turned to Frank.

"You've done well, Sheldon," he said, "and I'm sorry that you were hurt. You're relieved from duty for the rest of your watch. I'll put another man in your place. You'd better see the surgeons and have them wash out that cut of yours and bind it up again. Then tumble in and go to sleep. I hope you'll be all right in the morning."

Frank did as he was directed, and after the surgeon had dressed his wound and pronounced it not serious made his way to his bunk. He had to pass Rabig's bunk in reaching his own and he stopped there for a moment.

The place was dark, but he could see that the bunk was occupied, and from the snoring that arose from it the inmate seemed to be sleeping soundly.

Had he been mistaken?

CHAPTER XXII

THE SHADOW OF TREASON

When the soldiers jumped from their bunks the next morning at the call of the bugle Frank's comrades saw his bandaged head and they surrounded him at once with expressions of solicitude and alarm.

"What's the matter, old man?" asked Bart anxiously.

"Don't say you're badly hurt!" exclaimed Tom.

"You look all in," said Billy. "You're as pale as a ghost."

"I'm a long way from being a ghost yet," smiled Frank, as he drew on his clothes. "Wait till you see me tuck away the grub at breakfast. I butted my head against a stump last night to find out which was the harder, and the stump won."

"Stop your kidding and tell us about it," commanded Bart.

Frank told them the main features of his encounter of the night before, but it was only after mess when he had them by themselves that he voiced his suspicions of Rabig.

Tom gave a long whistle.

"That fellow will queer this whole outfit yet," he blurted out. "He's a sneak and a traitor. If he had his deserts he'd be up against the firing squad within twenty-four hours."

"Easy there, Tom," counseled Frank, looking around him, for in his excitement Tom had raised his voice. "Remember I'm not dead sure. I wouldn't swear to it in a court of law."

"Here comes Nick himself," remarked Bart.

"The Old Nick," growled Tom.

"Hello, Rabig," said Frank, as the former Camport bully came along.

Rabig grunted a surly "Hello" in reply, and was passing on when Billy hailed him.

"Sleep well, last night, Rabig?" he asked carelessly.

Rabig's face flushed and a frightened look came into his eyes.

"Sure I did," he snapped. "Why shouldn't I?"

"No reason in the world," replied Billy.

"These cool nights are fine for sleeping," remarked Tom. "A little too cool to be out in the woods, but just right for the trench."

Rabig seemed to be trying to think up a reply, but nothing came to him and he simply stood still and glowered at them. He appeared to be speculating. What significance was there in these apparently careless questions? Why should they be asked at all? How much did these cordially hated acquaintances of his really know?

"I hear that one of the Germans was killed close to our lines last night," said Billy, shifting the attack.

"Right inside our lines," corrected Tom. "And here's the fellow who shot him," pointing to Frank.

"Frank has nerve," drawled Billy.

Rabig shot a glare of hate that was not lost by the onlookers, who kept their eyes steadily on his face.

"He nearly got another one, too," observed Bart. "And the funny thing about it was that he thought he knew the fellow's voice."

This was coming too near for Rabig to pretend that he did not know what they were driving at. He turned upon them in desperation.

"Look here," he snarled viciously. "What do you fellows mean? If you mean that I'm mixed up in this thing you lie. Now don't you speak to me again or I'll make you sorry for it."

Without waiting for a reply he hurried off, and the four Camport chums looked after him with speculation in their eyes until he was lost to view at a turn of the trench.

"He's guilty all right," declared Tom with conviction.

"If ever guilt looked out of a man's eyes they looked out of his," agreed Bart.

"It seems so," admitted Frank with reluctance, "and yet he

was in his bunk when I went through last night." "How do you know it was Rabig?" Tom retorted. "Are you such a cute detective that you can tell one man's snore from another?"

"Who else could it have been?" asked Frank. "If it was some one else, that some one else must have been in cahoots with Rabig and agreed to make him seem to be in his bunk. I'd hate to think that there was more than one traitor in the regiment.

"One's more than enough," agreed Bart.

"What do you think we ought to do about it?" asked Billy.

"I don't know," replied Frank, with a worried look on his face. "It would be a terrible thing to accuse a man wrongfully of such a thing as treason. Rabig would simply deny it and put it up to us to prove it. Then, too, every one knows that there's no love lost between us and Nick, and they might think we were too ready to believe evil of him without real proof."

"On the other hand," replied Tom, "if we let him go on, we may wake up some time to find that Rabig has done the regiment more harm than a German battery could do."

"We'll simply have to keep our eyes peeled," was Billy's solution of the problem, "and watch that fellow like hawks. But if he makes one more bad break I don't think we ought to keep silent any longer. Let's hope that next time, if there is any next time, we'll have the goods on him so that there can't be any denying it."

But pleasanter thoughts diverted their attention just then, for the camp postman came into view and the boys rose with a whoop and pounced upon their letters. And all their spare time that morning was spent in reading and rereading the precious missives from their friends so many thousand miles away.

Frank was poring over a letter from his mother for the tenth time when he heard his name spoken and looked up to see Colonel Pavet, who was passing along in the company of another officer.

He had only a moment to spare, but that moment was given to Frank, who had risen and greeted him with a welcome as warm as his own.

"Ah, Monsieur Sheldon, letters from home, I see," he remarked. "I hope your mother is well."

"Very well, thank you," responded Frank. "And very grateful to you, Colonel Pavet, for the interest you have taken in her behalf and mine."

The colonel courteously waved the thanks aside.

He replied. "But you can tell Madame Sheldon that her affairs are progressing finely, though not as rapidly as they would if it were not for the distracted state of France. For instance, my brother Andre has been trying to get a furlough for a man who was formerly a butler in the De Latour family, and whose evidence he thinks will be most important in establishing your mother's right. It is only with the greatest difficulty that I have been able to bring this about, but I have succeeded at last, and the man will go to Auvergne next week to give his testimony. Let us hope that it will be as valuable as Andre thinks."

Again Frank expressed his thanks, and after a few more words they parted.

"Vive la France!" exclaimed Frank, as he saluted.

"Vive l'Amerique!" returned the colonel.

CHAPTER XXIII

A HAIL OF LEAD

"It's coming," declared Tom a few days later, as the boys were getting ready to go to mess.

"Listen to the oracle," mocked Bart.

"What's coming? Christmas?" inquired Billy.

"The big fight," replied Tom.

"Hear the general," gibed Bart.

"I've understood that Tom was General Pershing's right bower," put in Billy.

"They say he doesn't do a thing without him," said Bart.

"It's a pity that Tom didn't live in Napoleon's time," laughed Frank. "He'd have been a marshal sure."

"Napoleon," repeated Billy, with a faraway look in his eyes. "Where have I heard that name before?"

The four friends laughed as the comical scene in the little

French village rose up before them.

But with all their jesting they felt as sure as Tom that a big battle was impending. One did not have to be an officer to know that. The rank and file could tell it just as unerringly as their superiors.

For many days past all arms of the service had been working at top speed. Regiments and divisions had been reorganized and brought up to their full strength. Reserves had been brought from distant portions of the line and were massed heavily in the rear of the positions.

Raiding parties were active on both sides, as each was eager to get prisoners and information, and scarcely a night passed without heavy skirmishes between patrols that in former days would have risen to the dignity of battles.

Overhead the sky was dotted with the planes of the rival forces and the hum of the motors of the giant birds of prey was continuous. They fought not only in single combat but in sauacfrons, and the sight of one or more whirling down in flames was so common that it scarcely attracted attention.

And most ominous of all, the medical service was organizing gigantic units close to the front, in anticipation of the harvest of blood and wounds that was so close at hand.

Yes, a battle was coming. The grim reaper was sharpening his scythe and the watching world was waiting for the outcome in an agony of expectation.

The forces as far as known were evenly balanced, though it was rumored that the Germans were drawing large reserves temporarily from the eastern front, and color was lent to this by the fact that the Swiss frontier had been closed for a month to conceal the movement of troops.

It was not yet certain which side would make the first move. Each army was drawn up in a strong natural position with ranges of hills behind in the event of having to fall back.

"I hope we get in the first blow," remarked Frank, as he discussed the question with his chums.

"So do I," agreed Bart. "You know then where you're going to strike. This matter of fighting behind entanglements doesn't make a hit with me at all."

"There's more of a swing and rush to it when you attack," commented Billy. "Do you remember how it was, fellows, in that last big scrap when we were sprinting over No Man's Land? You're so eager to get at the Huns that you don't have time to think of danger."

But one foggy morning not long after, the German leaders settled the matter for the Camport strategists and struck with tremendous force at the Allied lines.

Two hours before dawn the German guns opened up with a roar that shook the earth. The air was full of flying shells; tear shells to blind the eyes of the Allied gunners so that they could not see to serve their pieces; mustard shells that bit into the lungs like a consuming fire; chlorine gas shells, with a deadly poison, to cause such agony that even surgeons, hardened in the exercise of their profession, turned away their faces from the writhings of the victims. Then, following these, a storm of leaden hail, withering, searing, blasting, before which it seemed no living thing could stand.

Crouched low in their trenches, massed line behind line, the Allied forces bent their heads to the storm, and waited in grim fury for the infantry attack that they knew would surely follow.

And it was not long in coming. The fog had risen by this time, and over the fields, rank upon rank, marching at the double quick, came masses of gray figures that seemed as endless as the waves of the sea.

The Allied artillery tore wide gaps in the dense masses, but they closed up instantly and continued their advance. Machine guns poured thousands of bullets into the living target, and the gunners served their pieces again and again until they were so hot that they burned the hand.

But true to their theory of warfare, the German leaders fed their men into the jaws of Moloch with cynical indifference. They had counted on paying a certain price, and they were willing to pay it.

But flesh and blood has its limitations, and before that murderous fire the ranks at last faltered.

Then from the trenches poured the Allied hosts in a fierce counter attack, and before their resistless charge the enemy wavered and at last broke. The gray lines melted away, and the ground, strewn with their dead and dying, was held by the Allied forces, which swiftly organized for the second attack, that they knew would not be long in coming.

CHAPTER XXIV

A DEED OF DARING

"We got them!" cried Bart, exultingly, as the boys worked feverishly at the preparations to meet the new attack.

"Right between the eyes," cried Billy.

"We drew first blood, all right," agreed Frank, "but they'll come again for more."

The prophecy was speedily realized, for again the enemy came forward, with undiminished ardor, protected this time by a deadly barrage fire behind which they marched with confidence. It was evident that this time the enemy, having tested the Allied mettle and found it excellent, had determined to place its chief reliance upon their big gun fire. And for a time it seemed as though their confidence was justified. The barrage fire swept the ground so completely that the Allies were forced to abandon their hastily seized positions in the open and retreat once more to the shelter of their trenches. But all the attacks of the German hordes, repeated again and again, were not able to get possession of those first line trenches, to which the Allies held with the fury of desperation. They were manned chiefly by the American troops, although certain units of French and

English held either end of the line. Again and again the storm broke, and again and again it was beaten back. The Germans had massed at that portion of the line numbers many times greater than those possessed by the defenders. By all the theories of war they ought to have been successful, but, like the old guard at Waterloo, the Americans might die, but would not surrender.

Yet after a while the very stubbornness of this resistance proved in itself a danger. On the right and the left the line, though not broken, was bent back. In this way the American position formed a salient in the German line, and was subjected to attack not only in front, but on the flanks. It became imperative that the line should draw back so that it might be in keeping with the position now held by the wings.

So, after hours of sanguinary fighting, the orders came to fall back, and the Americans, who had been standing like the army of Thomas at Chickamauga, fifty years previous, reluctantly obeyed, and fell slowly back to new positions, their faces always toward the foe.

"What kind of a fool stunt is this?" growled Tom, who, with his comrades, had been in the thick of the fight. "We had it all over those fellows, even if they were two or three times as many, and here we are retreating, when we ought to go ahead and lick the tar out of them." "Don't growl and complain, Tom," soothed Frank, whose left hand was bleeding where a bullet had zipped its way across it. "They'll get the licking all right when the time comes."

"It's good dope to give back a little sometimes," added Bart. "It's like boxing. When a blow comes straight at your stomach you bend back and that takes half the force away from the blow. Don't worry the least little bit about this fight. We may be bending a little, but we're not breaking, and before many hours we'll be standing the Heinies on their heads."

But the promise was not fulfilled that day, and when, night came after hours of tremendous struggle, the Allied forces had not regained their lost ground.

As darkness fell the combat lessened, and finally ceased altogether, as far as infantry attacks were concerned, although all through the night the artillery kept up a fire of greater or less intensity.

The boys of the regiment to which the Camport boys belonged were in rather a sober mood when they gathered around their field kitchens that night and partook of the food that was served out to them. They had not lost a gun, but they had yielded ground, and a great many of their comrades would never again answer the roll call. But their fighting spirit was at as high a pitch as ever, and they could scarcely wait till the morrow to get their revenge.

Frank and his chums had come through the day unscathed, except for the injury to Frank's hand and a mark across Billy's temple where a bullet had ridged the skin. Perhaps it was due to the fortune that is said to attend the brave, for they had borne themselves like heroes and had been stationed at one of the most fiercely battered portions of the line.

"I suppose they're gloating over this in Berlin to-night," said Tom gloomily, as they sat at the roots of a great tree whose bark and branches had been stripped from it by a storm of shells.

"And groaning over it in New York," added Billy.

"He laughs best who laughs last," said Bart. "To-morrow's a new day. Just watch our smoke."

"We'll eat 'em alive," prophesied Frank confidently, as he nursed his wounded hand. "Like John Paul Jones, we've just begun to fight."

"Do you fellows remember what General Corse said one time when Sherman asked him if he could hold out?" asked Bart.

"What was it?" asked Billy.

"He said: 'I've lost one eye and a piece of an ear, but I can lick a brigade or two yet,'" answered Bart.

"Good old scout," approved Billy, while the boys laughed.

"Well, we're not as badly off as that yet," said Frank, "although this hand of mine is smarting to beat the band."

"And my head is aching ready to split," added Billy. "One inch to the left and it would have been all up with your uncle Billy."

The fighting was resumed at dawn, and again it was the Germans who attacked. They had counted on their advantage of the day before to break the morale of their enemies and hoped by pressure to turn the withdrawal into a rout.

But like so many German calculations since the beginning of the war, they had figured badly. The Allies, stung by their discomfiture of the day before, fought like tigers. They beat the Germans back and took the offensive in their own hands.

The Germans retreated, though staunchly contesting every

foot of ground. In the front of Frank's company the enemy had established a machine gun nest that was particularly effective. Again and again the Americans sought to clean them out, but were met with such a galling fire that they lost heavily, and at last the captain decided that the guns were not worth the price he was paying to get possession of them. Yet the position would be of so much advantage, if captured, that he hesitated at changing his course and choosing another line of advance.

In the litter and wreck of the field, Frank's keen eye had caught sight of two big barrels filled with clothing for the troops. The barrels had been dropped from a wrecked motor lorry of a supply train. Like a flash an inspiration came to him.

He consulted a moment with Bart, whose eye lighted up as he nodded assent. Then he stepped up to his captain and saluted.

CHAPTER XXV

STORMING THE RIDGE

"What is it, Sheldon?"

"I think I can silence those guns, sir," Frank said.

A light came into the captain's eyes.

"How?" he asked.

In a few brief words Frank described his plan.

"But it's suicide," protested the captain. "There isn't one chance in a thousand that you'll come out alive."

"I know," said Frank. "But Raymond and I are willing to risk it if you give the word."

The captain pondered for a moment. It was a forlorn hope, but forlorn hopes sometimes won out.

"Go ahead," he said.

Frank nodded to Bart, and in a twinkling they had turned the big barrels over on their sides.

Then each lay on the ground behind his barrel and began to push it toward the enemy.

The men of their company had watched them wonderingly while they made their preparations, and when they realized what the boys had in mind they raised a thundering cheer that rose above the din of battle.

The crews of the two enemy machine guns looked with stupefaction at the big barrels coming toward them. Then they woke from their trance and a storm of bullets beat upon the barrels.

If they had been empty the bullets would have gone through and killed the boys behind them. But they were filled with woolen clothing, which while light enough to enable the boys to push the barrels with comparative ease was just the thing to stop the bullets. The whizzing missiles thudded into the clothing and there they stopped. It was on the same basis as the sandbag which stops a cannon ball that would go through an iron plate.

Steadily the boys kept on, pushing the barrels before them. They did not go on hands and knees, for then they would be exposed to the enemy bullets. It was a caterpillar motion, drawing their bodies along the ground, and was a tremendous tax on their muscles, for they could get no purchase.

One thing in their favor was that the ground sloped a trifle toward the enemy position and this made the barrels roll more easily.

By this time the enemy was growing frantic at this novel method of attack. They could not see their enemy, and they could not kill him. And the sight of those barrels coming toward them, as inexorably as fate, got on their nerves, already tense with the fury of the combat.

Nearer and nearer came the barrels to the guns until they were not more than twenty feet away. Then they stopped.

The German gunners drew fresh hope from this. Had their bullets found their mark in the bodies of their daring enemies?

But there were two very live boys behind those motionless barrels.

Frank and Bart had drawn a handful of grenades from their sacks. At a given signal they drew back their arms and hurled them over the barrels in quick succession.

They fell right in the midst of the machine guns. There was a tremendous explosion that killed some of the gunners and threw the rest into wild confusion.

"Now!" shouted Frank, and he and Bart leaped to their feet and rushed toward the guns.

There was a wild melee for a moment, and then the surviving Germans turned and ran in panic down the slope.

The boys slued the captured guns around and sent a stream of bullets after their wildly fleeing enemies.

The rout was complete, and the next minute the whole company, that had charged the instant the grenades were thrown, came tearing up, and there was a scene of hilarity and enthusiasm that passed description.

"The finest thing I ever saw!" declared the captain. "You boys are the stuff of which heroes are made."

But there was no time then to dwell on the exploit. The enemy was on the run and they must keep him going.

And they did, so well and so thoroughly, that when the day was over they had swept the whole ridge that had been their objective in the fight and planted Old Glory on its highest crest. And their victory was shared by the rest of the Allied line, who not only regained all the losses of the day before, but swept the Germans out of their first and second lines on a five-mile front, inflicting on them a defeat which they were long to remember.

And how the lesson that the Germans learned that day was repeated later on will be told in the next book of this series, entitled: "Army Boys on the Firing Line; Or, Holding Back the German Drive."

Not but what the victory had cost the Americans dearly. Every regiment engaged had its own long list of killed and wounded.

"Poor old Fred," said Frank, referring to Anderson. "His right arm was badly shattered and I'm afraid he may lose it."

"Fred is playing in hard luck," returned Bart. "That's twice he's been wounded. Remember the night down at the old mill when the bomb got his leg?"

"He's having more than his share," agreed Billy.

"There's Wilson, too," said Bart. "He's been in the thick of it all day, but he went down with a bullet in his shoulder just as we got to the top of the ridge."

"The corp certainly fought like a tiger," said Tom. "But he's worth a dozen dead men yet. A month in the hospital will fix him up all right, I hope."

"There's one good thing anyway," pat in Billy. "The Huns haven't taken many of our boys prisoners."

"And we've got more of their men than we know what to do with," exulted Frank.

"I know what I'd do with them," said Tom. "I'd send them to America to be imprisoned there and I'd put a bunch of them on every transport that sailed to the other side."

"That wouldn't be a bad stunt," agreed Bart. "Then if a submarine sank the ship it would carry a lot of their own people down to Davy Jones."

Among the missing was one whose loss did not greatly grieve the boys of the old Thirty-seventh. Nick Rabig did not answer to his name when the roll was called. They did not find his body on the field, nor was he among the wounded that were brought in and tenderly cared for in the hospitals.

"I see Nick is missing," remarked Frank to Bart later in the evening, as they were resting and rejoicing over the victory.

"Missing but not missed," put in the implacable Tom.

"If the Huns have got him, he'll feel more at home than he ever felt with us," remarked Bart.

"Maybe he was captured against his will," said Tom, "and then again *maybe*—"

"What do you suppose they'll say in Camport when they hear of this day's work, fellows?" asked Billy.

"Oh," answered Frank with a laugh, "they'll only say: 'It's nothing more than we expected.'"

"They know us, don't they?"

"Of course they do," broke in Tom. "We came to France to do our duty as American citizens, as well as soldiers."

"I wonder how long it will be before this war is over and we start for home?" came from Frank.

"Not tired of the game yet, are you?" quizzed Billy, quickly.

"Do I look as if I was tired of it?" was the counter-question.

"We are all going to stay over here until the Huns are licked good and proper!" burst cut Bart. "There is no use in stopping while the job is only half finished."

"Just you wait until Uncle Sam has a lot of men over here," put in Billy. "Then we'll show those Huns what's what and don't you forget it! We'll wallop them so thoroughly they'll be getting down on their knees yelling for mercy."

"Now you've said something!" came in a chorus from the others.

And here let us say good-bye to the Army Boys.

Friedrich Kerst
Friedrich Nietzsche
Fyodor Dostoyevsky
G.A. Henty
G.K. Chesterton
Gabrielle E. Jackson
Garrett P. Serviss
Gaston Leroux
George A. Warren
George Ade
Geroge Bernard Shaw
George Cary Eggleston
George Durston
George Ebers
George Eliot
George Gissing
George MacDonald
George Meredith
George Orwell
George Sylvester Viereck
George Tucker
George W. Cable
George Wharton James
Gertrude Atherton
Gordon Casserly
Grace E. King
Grace Gallatin
Grace Greenwood
Grant Allen
Guillermo A. Sherwell
Gulielma Zollinger
Gustav Flaubert
H. A. Cody
H. B. Irving
H.C. Bailey
H. G. Wells
H. H. Munro
H. Irving Hancock
H. R. Naylor
H. Rider Haggard
H. W. C. Davis
Haldeman Julius
Hall Caine
Hamilton Wright Mabie
Hans Christian Andersen
Harold Avery
Harold McGrath
Harriet Beecher Stowe
Harry Castlemon
Harry Coghill
Harry Houidini
Hayden Carruth
Helent Hunt Jackson
Helen Nicolay
Hendrik Conscience
Hendy David Thoreau
Henri Barbusse
Henrik Ibsen
Henry Adams
Henry Ford
Henry Frost
Henry James
Henry Jones Ford
Henry Seton Merriman
Henry W Longfellow
Herbert A. Giles
Herbert Carter
Herbert N. Casson
Herman Hesse
Hildegard G. Frey
Homer
Honore De Balzac
Horace B. Day
Horace Walpole
Horatio Alger Jr.
Howard Pyle
Howard R. Garis
Hugh Lofting
Hugh Walpole
Humphry Ward
Ian Maclaren
Inez Haynes Gillmore
Irving Bacheller
Isabel Cecilia Williams
Isabel Hornibrook
Israel Abrahams
Ivan Turgenev
J.G.Austin
J. Henri Fabre
J. M. Barrie
J. M. Walsh
J. Macdonald Oxley
J. R. Miller
J. S. Fletcher
J. S. Knowles
J. Storer Clouston
J. W. Duffield
Jack London
Jacob Abbott
James Allen
James Andrews
James Baldwin
James Branch Cabell
James DeMille
James Joyce
James Lane Allen
James Lane Allen
James Oliver Curwood
James Oppenheim
James Otis
James R. Driscoll
Jane Abbott
Jane Austen
Jane L. Stewart
Janet Aldridge
Jens Peter Jacobsen
Jerome K. Jerome
Jessie Graham Flower
John Buchan
John Burroughs
John Cournos
John F. Kennedy
John Gay
John Glasworthy
John Habberton
John Joy Bell
John Kendrick Bangs
John Milton
John Philip Sousa
John Taintor Foote
Jonas Lauritz Idemil Lie
Jonathan Swift
Joseph A. Altsheler
Joseph Carey
Joseph Conrad
Joseph E. Badger Jr
Joseph Hergesheimer
Joseph Jacobs
Jules Vernes
Julian Hawthrone
Julie A Lippmann
Justin Huntly McCarthy
Kakuzo Okakura
Karle Wilson Baker
Kate Chopin
Kenneth Grahame
Kenneth McGaffey
Kate Langley Bosher
Kate Langley Bosher
Katherine Cecil Thurston
Katherine Stokes
L. A. Abbot
L. T. Meade

L. Frank Baum
Latta Griswold
Laura Dent Crane
Laura Lee Hope
Laurence Housman
Lawrence Beasley
Leo Tolstoy
Leonid Andreyev
Lewis Carroll
Lewis Sperry Chafer
Lilian Bell
Lloyd Osbourne
Louis Hughes
Louis Joseph Vance
Louis Tracy
Louisa May Alcott
Lucy Fitch Perkins
Lucy Maud Montgomery
Luther Benson
Lydia Miller Middleton
Lyndon Orr
M. Corvus
M. H. Adams
Margaret E. Sangster
Margret Howth
Margaret Vandercook
Margaret W. Hungerford
Margret Penrose
Maria Edgeworth
Maria Thompson Daviess
Mariano Azuela
Marion Polk Angellotti
Mark Overton
Mark Twain
Mary Austin
Mary Catherine Crowley
Mary Cole
Mary Hastings Bradley
Mary Roberts Rinehart
Mary Rowlandson
M. Wollstonecraft Shelley
Maud Lindsay
Max Beerbohm
Myra Kelly
Nathaniel Hawthrone
Nicolo Machiavelli
O. F. Walton
Oscar Wilde

Owen Johnson
P.G. Wodehouse
Paul and Mabel Thorne
Paul G. Tomlinson
Paul Severing
Percy Brebner
Percy Keese Fitzhugh
Peter B. Kyne
Plato
Quincy Allen
R. Derby Holmes
R. L. Stevenson
R. S. Ball
Rabindranath Tagore
Rahul Alvares
Ralph Bonehill
Ralph Henry Barbour
Ralph Victor
Ralph Waldo Emmerson
Rene Descartes
Ray Cummings
Rex Beach
Rex E. Beach
Richard Harding Davis
Richard Jefferies
Richard Le Gallienne
Robert Barr
Robert Frost
Robert Gordon Anderson
Robert L. Drake
Robert Lansing
Robert Lynd
Robert Michael Ballantyne
Robert W. Chambers
Rosa Nouchette Carey
Rudyard Kipling
Saint Augustine
Samuel B. Allison
Samuel Hopkins Adams
Sarah Bernhardt
Sarah C. Hallowell
Selma Lagerlof
Sherwood Anderson
Sigmund Freud
Standish O'Grady
Stanley Weyman
Stella Benson
Stella M. Francis

Stephen Crane
Stewart Edward White
Stijn Streuvels
Swami Abhedananda
Swami Parmananda
T. S. Ackland
T. S. Arthur
The Princess Der Ling
Thomas A. Janvier
Thomas A Kempis
Thomas Anderton
Thomas Bailey Aldrich
Thomas Bulfinch
Thomas De Quincey
Thomas Dixon
Thomas H. Huxley
Thomas Hardy
Thomas More
Thornton W. Burgess
U. S. Grant
Upton Sinclair
Valentine Williams
Various Authors
Vaughan Kester
Victor Appleton
Victor G. Durham
Victoria Cross
Virginia Woolf
Wadsworth Camp
Walter Camp
Walter Scott
Washington Irving
Wilbur Lawton
Wilkie Collins
Willa Cather
Willard F. Baker
William Dean Howells
William le Queux
W. Makepeace Thackeray
William W. Walter
William Shakespeare
Winston Churchill
Yei Theodora Ozaki
Yogi Ramacharaka
Young E. Allison
Zane Grey

www.ingramcontent.com/pod-product-compliance
Lightning Source LLC
LaVergne TN
LVHW090606110826
845146LV00001B/280

9781421896502